KT-470-150

Mastering Business Planning and Strategy

The power of strategic thinking

Mastering Business Planning and Strategy

The power of strategic thinking

Paul Elkin

Published by

Thorogood Ltd

12-18 Grosvenor Gardens

London SW1W 0DH

0171 824 8257

A catalogue record for this book is available from the British Library

ISBN 1 85418 072 X (Trade edition)

ISBN 1 85418 190 4

© TMMi 1998

Printed in Great Britain by Ashford Colour Press

The author

Paul M Elkin

Paul is Managing Director of TMMi group, which provides consultancy services with a particular focus on business strategic development, performance management and corporate image. He is a Fellow of the Chartered Institute of Management Accountants and an experienced Management Consultant. After 15 years in a range of senior management roles in both public and private sector industry with UK and US businesses plus three years with Price Waterhouse, Management Consultancy Services, he formed the TMMi group at the end of 1989.

Paul's personal career and, in particular, recent consultancy experience have provided the opportunity to work with a wide range of UK, European and US-owned businesses. The nature of the involvement with each business has varied considerably according to their particular needs. Examples would include:

- Leading 'top team' workshops for directors/senior managers to consider strategic direction and key business issues

- Provision of consultancy expertise for the development of the business, its systems and its people

- Research and preparation of techniques and materials to support organisational change and development

- Development and implementation of a range of training and development initiatives including distance learning, management workshops, seminars and conferences.

He is actively involved with a number of leading corporates from a range of business sectors. Examples include AMEC Construction, BMW, Barclays Bank, Canon, Cow & Gate NUTRICIA, Logica and Xerox. Paul is the author of a series of practical 'reference guides' covering finance, strategy and business awareness and supports the delivery of MBA programmes in the areas of strategy and finance. He has also been involved in a range of initiatives in Europe for major corporates including ABB, Philips, International Paper and General Motors.

Contents

Icons

Throughout the Masters in Management series of books you will see references and symbols in the margins. These are designed for ease of use and quick reference directing you quickly to key features of the text. The symbols used are:

Key Question   Guide to Best Practice

Action Checklist   Key Learning Point

Activity   Key Management Concept

We would encourage you to use this book as a workbook, writing notes and comments in the margin as they occur. In this way we hope that you will benefit from the practical guidance and advice which this book provides.

Mastering
business success

....

Chapter 1

'Either lead, follow or get out of the way.'

Raymond G Viault
CEO, Jacobs Suchard

Content

Overview		Developing successful businesses
Business Goals ...	Q	What are the common aspirations of
the prime areas of focus		businesses?
	Q	What is the hierarchy of goals?
	Q	How are the goals integrated?
Business Success ...	Q	What are the key drivers of business
key drivers - the		success?
research evidence	Q	How well are these pursued?
	Q	How is achievement measured?
Business Stability ...	Q	What are the key drivers of business
avoiding failure - the		failure?
research evidence	Q	Where are the areas of focus to ensure
		stability?
	Q	How is achievement measured?

Achieving business stability and growth

Many directors and managers find their time completely occupied by 'fire-fighting', dealing with the crises and problems that are occurring today, rather than considering what is necessary to ensure the survival and eventual success of the business. Their skill and effort is absorbed in evaluating and taking tactical operational decisions whilst the business as a whole may be failing.

We need to recognise that this short term focus on dealing with today's issues is the natural response of many managers as:

- *That is what they have been 'trained' to do*

- *It is what is 'expected' of them*

- *They feel 'comfortable' taking these short term, often low risk, decisions.*

Successful businesses have rejected this type of management approach and instead developed people and an organisational culture that addresses the issues vital to success.

'He who has neither a thorough knowledge of his own conditions, nor the enemy's, is sure to lose in every battle.'

Sun Tzu - Chinese Warrior

Traditional review and planning systems within most organisations encourage an introverted, incremental approach to performance improvement. Leading businesses concentrate on three areas:

- **Customers:** how can we ensure that we satisfy customer needs?

- **Competitors:** how can we achieve and maintain competitive advantage?

- **Company:** how can we further develop and build on our company strengths?

Business leaders must ensure that they and their senior management teams apply the appropriate thinking processes. Traditionally managers all too often try to apply an 'operational' approach to problem solving and as a result are likely to constrain their thinking and limit their impact.

For example

The Production Director of a manufacturing company has been asked to examine opportunities for improving production performance. Over the last three years the production facilities have gradually improved output with the following results:

Utilisation of Productive Capacity

Year 1	71%
Year 2	75%
Year 3	78%

It has been suggested that improving the workload scheduling and concentration on longer production runs could reduce idle time. This is targeted to produce 81% utilisation of productive capacity.

In **Operational** terms this seems attractive giving a 10% improvement over four years ago.

However **Strategically** it is unlikely to achieve long term business success if major competitors are achieving 95% utilisation

An Operational response to a Strategic Problem

Those businesses whose strengths are solely in their operational ability – and surviving in a game where the margins are narrow – tend to be *efficiency* driven. In other words doing what they have always done, only trying to do it better.

Strategies for success are about being more *effective*, in terms of identifying what it is that the business should be doing today and tomorrow in order to survive and prosper in the long run.

In the following pages we will examine the key issues related to business success and identify some initial techniques for analysing the performance of the organisation.

Business goals

Normally each corporate has specific goals it is consistently pursuing. These vary between organisations but the table below is a summary of common business goals identified by research.

Key Learning Point

	Per cent
Profitability	89
Growth	82
Market share	66
Employee welfare	62
Product quality and service	60
Research and development	54
Expansion outside core business	51
Efficiency	50
Financial stability	49
Management development	35

Source : McKinsey

The per cent column indicates what proportion of the corporates surveyed were explicitly pursuing this goal.

In reality the table is a mixture of goals and success factors which are important to the achievement of those goals. True goals are probably confined to the first three categories.

- Profitability
- Growth
- Market share

Of these three the one of primary importance to commercial businesses would be profitability – the reason why most enterprises exist! From an owner's or corporate parent perspective this could be more specifically defined as Return. Growth and Market Share are pursued to the extent that they yield a long–term benefit in terms of Return. In simple terms the measure Return reflects the relationship between the profit generated and the money tied–up in the business represented by the assets of that business. This starts to identify a series of three linked financial criteria that provide the framework for results management in the business:

Return	=	**Margin**	x	**Utilisation**
Profit		Profit		Sales
————	=	————	x	————
Assets		Sales		Assets

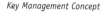

Key Management Concept

The paramount goal for most businesses is Return. However, within the business, managers are focused on achievement in the two constituent areas of margin and utilisation, with specific targets relevant to their area of responsibility. Examples would include those shown on the next page:

Margin

Sales management	–	gross margin achievement
	–	pricing and discounting
	–	sales expense control
Production management	–	production cost
	–	purchase price
	–	labour cost

Utilisation

Sales management	–	credit terms and debtor collection
Production management	–	stock level and turnover
	–	labour efficiency

If the business provides a framework of operational margin and utilisation controls it is implicitly focusing on the key elements that drive return – the paramount goal.

Business goals — a natural hierarchy

RETURN
=
MARGIN × UTILISATION

GROWTH AND MARKET SHARE

PRODUCT QUALITY AND SERVICE
EMPLOYEE WELFARE   RESEARCH + DEVELOPMENT
EFFICIENCY

Business success – the evidence

This section summarises from research evidence a number of key drivers of business success. These should be used as a leadership checklist to ensure that the business is clearly focused on, and actively pursuing, these foundations for long term business health.

Concept

The highly competitive nature of many markets and the likely future prospect of continued economic turbulence as national and global economic fortunes vary, requires that business managers continue to look for opportunities to improve performance. This will primarily be achieved by improving effectiveness in the areas of winning/retaining customers, developing organisational competence and financial control.

It is vital not to lose sight of the fact that research reveals that...

'... Nothing fails like success'

This is the paradox facing many businesses particularly successful ones!

Research into the top performing UK businesses has identified a number of common 'Success Factors'. These are briefly summarised below:

Leadership

- Experienced leadership with a thorough understanding of the business and the market /segment in which it operates.

Maintaining the 'Small Company Culture'

- Good employee relationships supported by good pay/incentives
- Close links and strong loyalty.

Key Management Concept

Quality focus

- Customers have a strong perception of quality

- Close contact with customers, excellence of customer handling and a thorough understanding of needs.

Market driven

- Ingenuity and innovation in product and service delivery

- Good market intelligence identifying what customers want

- High investment in R+D type activities and brand development.

Profit focus

- More interested in profitability than simple growth in sales volume or sales value, or market share

- Good management systems to clearly identify true performance and profitability.

Control of borrowings

- Avoidance of borrowing unless essential for business development.

Source: Coopers / KMPG

Application

These success drivers are obvious <u>but</u> it is amazing how many businesses ignore their importance. This is particularly true in difficult markets or economic recession where short term financial constraints lead to cost cutting. Early casualties are staff levels, training, research, product innovation, 'non–essential' customer care etc. These are targeted because they produce relatively easy short term cost reduction. Ironically they often also reduce the ability of the business to respond to and satisfy customer needs and expectations. In practical terms the business has reduced its capability to win and retain customers at a time when there are fewer customers in the market and it is even more important to win the sale. Consider the following questions:

- Are these success factors relevant to your business?
- What systems do you have to measure your effectiveness (and that of competitors) in each area?
- What systems should you have to measure your effectiveness?
- What level of achievement do you truly have on each factor?
- What are the implications for the future development and stability of the business?

Action Checklist

Business stability – the evidence

The previous section identified a number of factors that support business success. This section takes a different perspective and is based upon research into the common factors underlying the failure of businesses both large and small. This identifies a series of principles vital to promote organisational stability and reduce risk.

Concept

Business research has identified the following key factors for business stability:

Management style

- The management approach must be relevant to the commercial requirements of the marketplace and the situation of the business. A different approach will be required dependant on the boom or recessionary nature of the market sector and the general economy.

Concentration on 'core business'

- No interest in diversification unless this is clearly linked to the business and yields direct cost or competitive advantage.

Control of costs and resources

- Consistently pursuing cost reduction/efficiency initiatives
- Not delaying taking action – 'grasping the nettle'.

Key Management Concept

Understanding 'product/service' profitability

- A clear and accurate understanding of the actual profit generated by different 'products/services'
- Appropriate systems to identify actual costs and profitability recognition that being busy may not be the same as being profitable.

Control of 'working capital'

- Rigorous management of stocks, work–in–progress and debtors to ensure the minimum of finance tied–up.

Maintenance of realistic stock values

- Valuation of all stocks at the true value (lower of cost or realisable value)
- Appropriate stock liquidation, write–down and obsolescence write–off procedures.

Cash forecasting

- Thorough cash forecasting and good management of cash flow.

Source : TMMp / Barclays

Application

In the same way as the previous section 'business success' it is vital to address the five fundamental questions.

Action Checklist

- Are these factors relevant to your business?

- What systems do you have to measure your effectiveness (and that of competitors) in each area?

- What systems should you have to measure your effectiveness?

- What level of achievement do you truly have on each factor?

- What are the implications for the future development and stability of the business?

Mastering strategic analysis

Chapter 2

*'To win every battle by actual fighting before
a war is won, it is not the most desirable.
To conquer the enemy without resorting to war is the most desirable.*

*The highest form of generalship is to conquer the enemy by strategy.
The next highest form of generalship is to conquer the enemy by alliance.
The still next highest form of generalship is to conquer the enemy by battles.
The worst form of generalship is to conquer the enemy by besieging walled cities.'*

Sun Tzu
Chinese Warrior
The Art of War

Content

Overview	An introduction to a structured approach and the analysis of the corporate environment to identify the challenges and opportunities facing the organisation.

Environmental Mapping

Q   What are the characteristics of the environment(s) in which the business operates?
Q   How are the key factors changing?
Q   What will be the impact on future strategic choices?

Industry Mapping

Q   What is the nature and intensity of competition?
Q   Where does the bargaining power rest in the industry?
Q   What threatens to destabilise the industry?

Key Question

SWOT Analysis

Q   What are the current strengths and weaknesses?
Q   What are the future opportunities and threats?
Q   How should we evaluate the impact?

From → To analysis

Q   Where are we now?
Q   Where do we want to be?
Q   What are the potential consequences of the changes?

Root Cause Analysis

Q   What are the key challenges or problems?
Q   What are the underlying issues?
Q   Where should change action be focused?

Mastering Strategic Analysis - the Business Objectives

- Defining changes in the industry dynamics and stability

- Identifying the challenges facing the corporate and its senior executives

- Focusing attention on the responses required to promote future security and success

Overview

Strategy is the process of deciding how to best position the organisation in its competitive environment in order to achieve and sustain competitive advantage, profitably. Strategy is formed at both corporate level (what industries/markets should we operate in) and business unit level (in what segments should we compete – and how). This chapter will focus on corporate level strategic considerations.

The pace of change has significantly increased in recent years and the competitive arena has enlarged, driven by, for example, larger international corporates with an appetite for new markets, reduced barriers to international trade, and technology. The following summarises some of the key 'shifts'.

Changing focus of corporate strategy

From	To
Relatively static economies	Shifting unstable economies
Durable products	Shortening product life cycles
Stable customer needs	Escalating customer demands
Market focus	Segment focus
National/regional markets	Global markets
Ownership of technology	Freedom of access to technology

Strategic focus: 'chess'	**Strategic focus: 'interactive video game'**
War of position (strength)	War of movement (stealth)
Build market share	Create segmented dominance
Defensive	Offensive
Reputation and strength	Competence and responsiveness

The process of *strategic analysis* is one of focusing down 'layer by layer' to develop a clear understanding of the factors which effect the corporate and the market in which it operates. It may therefore be referred to as the 'onion skin' approach, as illustrated below. Each layer must in turn be 'peeled off' and analysed before the core Strategic Business Unit (SBU) element is approached. The subsequent chapter *Mastering Market Analysis* will examine the practical approaches to SBU appraisal and future planning.

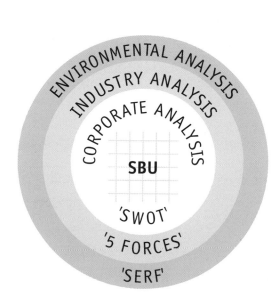

Environmental mapping

This technique is intended to capture the key characteristics of the environment in which the business operates. These factors, which may be supportive or constraining to the future development of the organisation, provide the 'back-cloth' against which the future strategies and plans must be formulated.

Concept

Key Management Concept

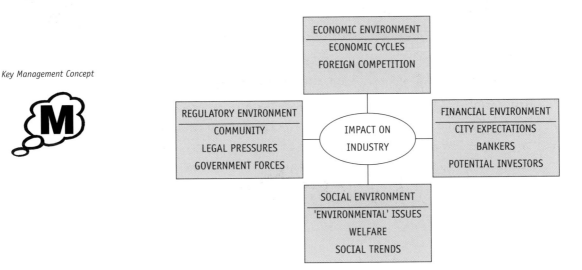

The model analyses the environment into four areas of focus. It should be used flexibly to reflect the nature of the relevant country/market environment. This means that for a large corporate, with a significant spread of operations, it is appropriate to separately map the different environments in which the various parts of the organisation operate. A 'generic' analysis may be too broad to be accurate and useful.

Application

The facts are normally identified by the senior management of the business from their personal knowledge and experience. Naturally this assumes that they have sufficient background in the environment to generate accurate data. If this experience does not exist external information sources would need to be used to supplement the existing knowledge of the business. Even where knowledge is 'strong' it is prudent to validate key facts/assumptions and to compare alternative views of the future.

Action Checklist

The analysis should be used to identify:

- The general pressures and constraints which surround the industry in which the business operates

- The principle expectations of each environmental group

- The issues that are dominant and are likely to exert the most pressure or influence on the future direction and prospects of the corporate. This is often achieved by using H/M/L (High/Medium/Low) categorisation of each factor.

Industry mapping

This is a model that enables the competitive environment in which the organisation operates to be analysed. It was developed by Michael Porter and is often referred to as the 'Porter 5 Forces' model. It helps to identify the strength of the competitive forces that impact on the industry. Whereas the previous stage 'Environmental Mapping' examined more generally the wider commercial context affecting all industries, this approach is focused on the specific industry in which the organisation operates.

Concept

Key Management Concept

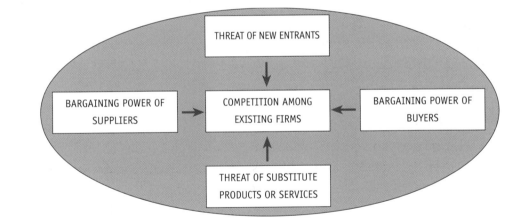

The model identifies five industry forces that directly influence an organisation.

Competition among existing firms – this is the natural competitive rivalry which exists between the various businesses operating within the industry marketplace.

Threat of new entrants – this is the potential likelihood of, and ease of, entry for new firms into the market. An example would be the entry of Japanese contractors into the UK construction market.

Threat of substitute products or services – this is where a product or service, perhaps produced through a different technology, enters the market. An example would be the entry of compact discs into the audiotape/record market – providing the same product, 'music', through a different technology.

Bargaining power of suppliers – this examines the relationship between businesses in the industry and the suppliers to those businesses. Where suppliers have a unique or restricted availability product they can exert a strong influence over prices and conditions of supply, therefore potentially putting pressures on the businesses purchasing their product/services.

Bargaining power of buyers – this examines the relationship between businesses in the industry and the customers of those businesses. The purpose is to identify the relative strength of the business in the customer relationship.

Application

The objective is to consider the industry marketplace and to identify the ability of each 'force' to de-stabilise the existing situation. The power of the influence on the business of each force can then be ranked (often using a 'H' high/'M' medium/'L' low categorisation). This enables appropriate actions to be considered to take advantage of, or defend, the situation to be reflected in the strategy and plans of the organisation.The following paragraphs summarise some of the key factors related to each of the five forces.

Action Checklist

Competition among existing firms is a powerful force if:

- Competitors are equally balanced
- Market/industry growth is slow or negative
- Fixed costs are high
- Buyers can easily switch purchasing between businesses without penalty
- Capacity is increased only in large increments which means that utilisation (and therefore volume) is critical
- The market/industry is strategically important to the businesses.

Threat of new entrants is a powerful force when:

- There are low economics of scale (i.e. volume/size do not significantly change the cost base)
- Customer loyalty is low
- Products/services are 'commodities' with little differentiation
- Capital spend is low
- Defensive retaliation is minimal
- Low technological, regulatory or competence barriers exist.

Threat of substitute products or services is a powerful force when:

- The price/performance trade-off is good in comparison to the established product/service
- Buyers can easily switch purchasing to the substitute without penalty
- Buyer acceptability of substitutes is high.

Bargaining power of suppliers is a powerful force when:

- There is a limited number of suppliers or availability of supply
- The industry is unimportant as a customer for the supplier
- The supplier's product is an important input
- The supplier's product is valuably differentiated
- There is a threat of forward integration
- There are high costs of switching to an alternative supply.

Bargaining power of buyers is a powerful force when:

- There are a limited number of buyers
- The purchases represent a significant proportion of the buyers costs
- Products/services are 'commodities' with little differentiation
- There is ease of switching to alternative suppliers
- There is a threat of backward integration
- The purchases are of low importance
- The buyer has full information on costs and performance.

The following summary framework can be helpful for evaluating the Porter 5 Forces analysis.

Key factors	Influence +/0/-	Impact H/M/L	Consequences
Competitor rivalry			
New entrants			
Substitutes			
Suppliers			
Buyers			

For each of the five competitive forces:

- **Identify the key factors** associated with that force
- **Evaluate the influence** of that factor on the industry/business as positive (+), neutral (0) or negative (-)
- **Evaluate the impact** of that factor – how critical it is to future success and stability – as high (H), medium (M) or low (L)
- **Summarise the consequences** for the industry/business together with any potential action themes which need to be considered.

Illustrative action themes could include:

Competition among existing firms

- Differentiate to strengthen competitive advantage
- Strengthen brand to improve loyalty/retention
- Re-segment the market
- Aggressively reduce cost base to improve competitive strength
- Acquire competitors to improve market position
- Develop strategic alliances.

Threat of new entrants

- Build entry barriers
- Vigorously defend any early entry
- Consider attacking potential new entrants 'on their own ground'.

Threat of substitute products or services

- Continuously research potential substitutes
- Re-engineer and continuously improve existing products/services to ensure performance
- Evaluate opportunity to invest in substitute industry/technology
- Monitor customer preferences and understand changing requirements.

Bargaining power of suppliers

- Research alternative suppliers
- Build advantageous 'preferred supplier' relationships
- Re-assess requirements and re-engineer to reduce 'lock-in' to specialists
- Evaluate opportunity for backward integration.

Bargaining power of buyers

- Segment customer base and focus on most valuable

- Emphasise relationship management and supplementary support to enhance loyalty

- Develop image/brand strength to enhance preference in purchasing decisions

- Evaluate opportunity for forward integration

- Appraise customer business to understand market/industry context in which purchase decisions are taken.

Summary – responding to the characteristics

Examination of the industry and market in which the organisation operates is a vital initial stage of corporate strategic review and subsequent business unit planning. This industry mapping approach using the 'Porter 5 Forces' model...

... focuses on the structure of the industry/market

... examines the key forces driving overall profitability and stability, identifying

- what forces now exist

- how these forces are likely to change

- the potential attractiveness

- the primary risk factors

... draws attention to the strategic issues and challenges facing the companies operating in that industry/segment

... starts to highlight the strategic direction and action themes for corporate development.

The analysis process is equally important for evaluation of any new strategic opportunity as well as existing business operations.

The structure of the industry will significantly effect the profit potential of the business operating in that industry. The strategy and actions of a business operating in the industry may improve or destroy the industry structure. Each business (and the relevant decision takers) must recognise and evaluate the impact, short term and long term, of actions taken on the overall industry structure and attractiveness.

SWOT analysis

SWOT is a widely used thinking framework for identifying Strengths, Weaknesses, Opportunities and Threats. It enables key factors to be visibly recorded as a high level summary of a business (or personal) situation. It is a summary that is simple but powerful. The technique is commonly used by consultants to document the key factors arising from the review of a particular project or business.

Concept

Key Management Concept

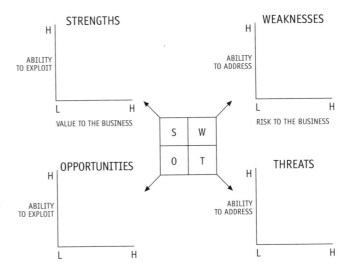

The use of SWOT enables an assessment to be made of the overall internal state of a business and the direction in which it is heading, through looking at its Strengths and Weaknesses. It also enables a judgement to be made about aspects of the external business environment, which can affect the performance of the business, through looking at the Opportunities and Threats it faces in the wider world.

Application

The SWOT summary may be used to consolidate key issues identified through other forms of analysis already highlighted in this chapter (e.g. environmental mapping, industry mapping, etc.) However, the following are illustrative of the types of questions that should additionally be covered.

Strengths and Weaknesses

Action Checklist

Money

Q   What is the cash and profit performance of the business?

Q   How sensitive is the business to a change in the level of demand?

Q   What are the levels of fixed and variable costs?

Q   At what level of activity does the business fail to break-even (i.e. cover its costs and its cash commitments)?

Management

Q   What is the management and organisational structure?

Q   Does it meet the needs of the business?

Q   What is the general level of manager's skills, their level of expertise, drive and energy?

Q   What is the leaders/owners philosophy – why are they in the business?

Q   What is the business strategy and plan?

Staff

Q   What is the quality of the people employed?

Q   How good are team relationships?

Q   How well are people motivated and rewarded?

Equipment

Q   What is the current state of plant, workshop equipment, handling equipment etc?

Q   What is the replacement policy?

Q   Is the policy being actively implemented?

Q   How well utilised are the facilities?

Q   What is the level of output quality achieved?

Premises

Q   What is the condition of the premises?

Q   How suitable are they for present/future needs?

Q   What is their location?

Q   What alternative uses are there for the site/premises and what is the impact on realisable value?

Stock

Q   What levels of stocks are held – what is the stockholding policy?

Q   What are the stock turn performances?

Q   What are the levels of work-in-progress?

Q   Is too large a proportion of capital tied up in stocks and WIP?

Q   Are there redundant/obsolete stocks?

Q   What influence does the company have over supplier's prices?

Q   What is the mix of business?

Q   What are the volumes sold and what is the profit margin performance?

Q   How secure is the customer base?

Q   What is the trend of customer satisfaction performance?

Marketing

Q   What is the penetration of the market?

Q   What are the competitive advantages – how does the business differentiate itself from the competition?

Q   What is the customer profile?

Q   Who are the main competitors?

Q   What is the state of the market?

Q   What is the level of customer loyalty?

Q   What influence do customers have over prices?

Financial

Q   How well informed are the management team about the financial position of the business?

Q   How relevant and accurate is the financial information produced?

Q   Are the financial systems and controls in operation adequate?

Q   How well prepared/accurate are the business plans, budgets and forecasts?

Opportunities and Threats

Competitiveness

Q How intense is the competition?

Q Are there new competitors likely to enter the market?

Q How secure is the position of the business in the market?

Technological changes

Q How will changing technology affect the business – products and processes?

Social changes

Q What effect will changing life-styles have on the business and product mix?

Q How will these affect employees/managers/customers?

Political changes

Q What will be the impact of changes in government policy or changes at the wider European level?

Taxation changes

Q To what extent is the business likely to be vulnerable to new or changing taxes?

Economic changes

Q What will be the likely impact on the business of inflation recession or an increase in interest rates?

Legislative changes

Q How likely are potential legislative changes (either domestic and/ or European) to affect the business?

From ⟹ To analysis

This technique helps to simplify strategic choices to enable clear executive decisions to be evaluated and taken. It contrasts existing and potential future characteristics of the organisation and encourages evaluation of the consequences of alternative actions.

Concept

The diagram below illustrates a simplified From ⟹ To analysis and the potential consequences which could arise from the change.

From ⟹ To analysis

From ⟹	To	Consequences
Production led ⟹	Market led	Better market intelligence required
		Stronger customer focus
		Reduced production efficiency
Functional structure ⟹	Business unit structure	Better results focus
		Recruitment of general managers
		Reduced functional co-ordination
		Change in reporting systems
		Sales force division
Poor customer support ⟹	Outstanding customer support	Salesforce reorganisation
		Appointment of technical support team
		Training
		Additional costs
		Improved customer retention
		Increased sales

Key Management Concept

Application

The approach is usually linked to the other strategic analysis tools highlighted in this book. The From ⟹ To factors may well emerge from the previously mentioned Environmental Analysis, Industry Analysis and SWOT, and are a summary of certain of the key challenges facing the organisation.

The consequences of each From ⟹ To change should be highlighted, both positive and negative. Based on this, some broad decisions can be taken to pursue, or not pursue, certain strategies. The transition From ⟹ To is an option and the decision not to change may be taken in some circumstances where the cost/benefit balance of the consequences is not attractive.

Root cause analysis

This is a simple problem diagnosis technique, which provides a visual map of the factors that contribute to a particular organisational issue. The purpose of this analysis is to establish the root cause(s) of the problem. The technique is sometimes called fishbone analysis

Concept

The following is an illustration of how the approach can be used to identify a series of underlying factors, which contribute to a problem.

Root cause analysis

Action Checklist

Application

Initially the problem is clearly stated on the right hand side – this is the effect. The primary areas that contribute to the problem are then identified. In this example these are :

- Marketing – the advertising and promotion of the product/service
- Qualifying – the selection of potential telephone contacts
- Systems – the approach to rewarding performance
- Staff – the quality, availability and capability of the tele-sales team.

The individual causes are identified by those who have direct experience of the problem. This normally takes place in a brainstorming type session to build up a detailed picture of the circumstances.

The causes can be prioritised according to their seriousness. Those that are complex and/or serious may then be individually analysed further using the same technique.

The overall objective is to build up a clear picture of the situation to highlight areas of specific attention for problem solving.

Mastering
market analysis

· ·

Chapter 3

'The management of change is both difficult and time-consuming, the more so if a company's leadership and strategies have been successful in the past. However, we have found at Grand Metropolitan that if time and resources are invested in developing a clear 'vision' – that is, in defining a company's ambition in terms of the role it will play, the geographic and market sectors in which it will compete, and the sustainable competitive advantage it has or can achieve, as well as the distinctive skills that will make it successful and resilient – then this creates a major integrating force which can help leadership overcome barriers to change, channels the energy of management to strive towards their highest aspirations, and positions the company to exploit strategic opportunities.'

Sir Allen Sheppard, Chairman,
Grand Metropolitan plc

Content

Overview		An introduction to the thinking processes that support the analysis of market position, identification of alternative competitive strategies and directional choice
Market Mapping	Q	Who are our primary competitors?
	Q	What is our relative market position?
	Q	What changes are occurring?
Strategic Business Unit (SBU) Analysis	Q	What segments of the market do we operate in?
	Q	What segments of the market should we operate in?
	Q	What are the key drivers of success?
Competitor Profiling	Q	How do we perform on each of the key drivers of success?
	Q	How do our competitors perform on each of the key drivers of success?
	Q	Where are the gaps, positive and negative?
Directional Policy Matrix - SBU Attractiveness	Q	How commercially attractive are the businesses in which we operate?
	Q	Where are the market opportunities and risks?
	Q	What strategic direction is appropriate for each SBU?
Competitive Positioning - Generic Strategies	Q	What are the primary drivers of competitive advantage?
	Q	What should be our strategy for achieving competitive advantage?
	Q	What do we need to do well to successfully pursue our strategy?
Competitive Positioning - Differentiation	Q	What are the alternative bases of differentiation?
	Q	How are we actually differentiated from our competitors?
	Q	How should we be differentiated from our competitors?

Overview – defining business unit strategy

The previous chapter '*Mastering strategic analysis*' focused on understanding the corporate, the industry in which it is positioned and the wider environment in which the industry operates. As a foundation for this chapter it is important to introduce two definitions :

Corporate strategy

- *This is concerned with the organisation as a whole. It defines the industries/markets in which the corporate will operate and sets the direction in terms of development of the overall portfolio. It will provide the basis for the allocation of resources.*

Business unit strategy

- *This is concerned with the component parts of the organisation (Strategic Business Units). It defines how the business will compete in the market in which it operates and how it will be positioned in relation to its competitors.*

This chapter deals in some depth with how the business positions its offerings (products/services) versus those of its competitors. This analysis and planning process <u>must</u> be applied at Strategic Business Unit (SBU) level. Too often market strategies are evaluated and set at too high a level (corporate) which leads to a poor fit – or no fit! – with the real dynamics of the individual market segments in which the SBU operates. Too often market managers and business unit directors challenge strategic decisions saying '*this approach won't work in our market*'. In most cases they are identifying the fundamental flaw in the strategic review and business planning processes pursued by many corporates. Briefly, the analysis and decision taking process is simply pitched too high up the organisation. It deals with broad markets and corporate direction, rather than the individual market segments and different competitive areas in which the business really operates. The result is bland, ill-fitting, strategies that fail to achieve the desired outcomes.

Market analysis – the process

The following pages link a series of practical tools to provide a structured market analysis and action planning process.

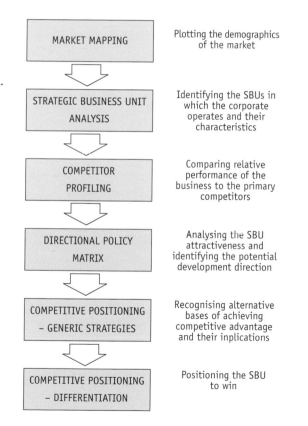

MARKET MAPPING	Plotting the demographics of the market
STRATEGIC BUSINESS UNIT ANALYSIS	Identifying the SBUs in which the corporate operates and their characteristics
COMPETITOR PROFILING	Comparing relative performance of the business to the primary competitors
DIRECTIONAL POLICY MATRIX	Analysing the SBU attractiveness and identifying the potential development direction
COMPETITIVE POSITIONING – GENERIC STRATEGIES	Recognising alternative bases of achieving competitive advantage and their inplications
COMPETITIVE POSITIONING – DIFFERENTIATION	Positioning the SBU to win

Market analysis – the business objectives

- *Selecting markets and market segments in which to compete*
- *Providing a mix of products and services that customers value*
- *Doing it better and/or at lower cost than the competitors.*

Market analysis – setting competitive strategy

The structured market analysis process is a core element of the overall approach to strategic review and business planning coverage of this book. The 'corporate mindset' often defines this process as an annual or periodic exercise. However markets are dynamic not static with the pace of change increasing in many sectors. This requires that:

- These strategic thinking processes become a continuous focus of management being integrated into the ongoing disciplines of review and decision taking
- Factual evidence is routinely and rigorously appraised to avoid decisions being based on subjective beliefs about competitor positioning and customer relationships.

Fundamental principles are:

- Focus on how the business positions itself in the eyes of the customers who choose between offerings
- Markets are dynamic, not static therefore market analysis is a process not an event
- Customers decisions are based on:
  - relative benefits <u>not</u> benefits
  - perceptions <u>not</u> facts.

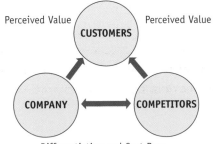

Perceived Value   Perceived Value

CUSTOMERS

COMPANY ⟷ COMPETITORS

Differentiation and Cost Base

Market mapping

This module introduces certain concepts for creating a 'map' of the marketplace in which the firm operates. The purpose is to examine the relative position and strength of the business versus the competition.

Concept

The following are illustrative visual 'maps' which are helpful in understanding the dynamics of the market. Each circle represents a company.

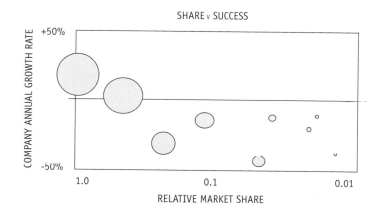

This 'map' identifies the degree to which market share is a driver of company growth. Relative market share is the size of each firm's share expressed as a proportion of the share held by the market leader. The market leader share is therefore shown as 1.0 on the left-hand axis of the graph. In this example it can be observed that only those businesses with a dominant/strong market share are achieving positive growth.

Key Management Concept

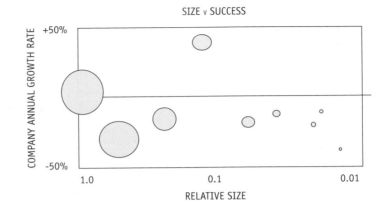

This second 'map' examines the correlation between relative size of the business (defined as annual turnover) and company growth. This reveals that in this market both large and small businesses are failing to grow whilst one medium size player is bucking the trend and achieving high growth.

These two analyses help to build-up a general picture of the market in which the business operates and the relative fortunes of the competitors. Different markets and products will have a different relationship between the key factors of market share, size and growth. It is important to understand these relationships, and how they are changing over time, as part of the input to business development planning.

The following graphical presentation highlights the actual performance of each competitor, this time from the perspective of the customer.

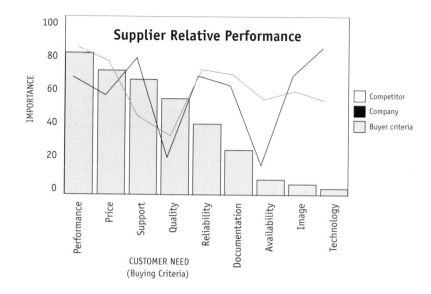

The vertical bars represent the relative importance of each factor to the customer. This is normally established through customer research undertaken to provide the basis for customer satisfaction monitoring. The lines track the latest performance of the firm and the key competitor(s) against these buying criteria. These may be established from customer surveys, customer clinics or independent market research. This reveals any negative (or positive) gaps in relative performance. Gaps are obviously of more significance where the buying criteria is of more importance to the customer.

Application

These three 'maps' enable a clearer picture to be established of the characteristics of the market in which the firm operates and the relative strength of the customer relationship. The key questions are:

Action Checklist

Q What is our relative market share? – and how is this changing?

Q Who is achieving growth? – and how?

Q What are our customer needs? – and what is their relative importance?

Q What level of customer satisfaction are we achieving against each need?

Q What level of customer satisfaction are our competitors achieving against each need?

Q Where are the performance gaps: positive and negative?

Strategic Business Unit (SBU) analysis

Organisations are often complex and it is necessary to break down the overall corporate into Strategic Business Units (SBUs) for plans to be clearly focused and effective. Unless these SBUs are identified any planning will be generic and bland – therefore unlikely to produce the desired positive results.

Concept

The approach uses a 'Customer – Offering Matrix'. Each cell within the matrix is an actual or potential relationship between a customer group and an offering category. Where the relationship is significant (or of significant potential) this is a SBU which needs to be individually considered for planning purposes.

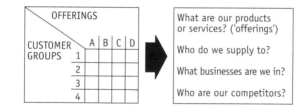

Key Management Concept

Application

Strategic planning must focus individually on each SBU to define clearly targeted goals and actions. The approach to the development (or disposal) of each SBU is likely to be different, reflecting the specific nature of the customer relationship, the competitive environment and the key factors for successful development.

Action Checklist

For each cell, or relationship, the following should be identified :

- The customer requirements
- The primary competitors
- The competitive process.

This will identify the various bases on which new business is won from competitors (i.e. how differentiation is achieved) and the primary factors which are important to maintaining existing customer loyalty/satisfaction.

Using these facts it is now possible to take each significant SBU (cell in the matrix) and to define those things which the business needs to do well - these are referred to as Critical Success Factors (CSFs). The CSFs are a vital input to strategic planning and objective setting. They help to clarify what competencies the organisation requires and implications for the type of structure that is appropriate.

If we take an example of a Strategic Business Unit which may be defined as a bank offering lending products to small business customers. The major competitors would be other lending banks and the competitive rivalry would be intense. The customer requirements, expressed in order of importance, would be:

- Understanding my business
- Cost (price/rate)
- Understanding my needs

- Consistent/reliable service
- Continuity of primary contact
- Speed of response
- Value for money
- Speed of supply (availability of funding)
- Quality of primary contact
- Competitive terms of trade (arrangement fees/security fees etc).

Illustrative critical success factors (CSF) and related consequences would be:

CSF	Consequences
Prime contact quality and continuity	Appointment of relationship managers with high personal credibility Business/ commercial awareness training of relationship managers, including needs identification skills
Price competitiveness	Strong cost control and efficiency Effective lending risk assessment and margin management
Competitor awareness	Structured competitor intelligence gathering Lost customer analysis
Service responsiveness, accuracy & quality	Reliable systems Development and motivation of support staff Highly developed customer awareness

So far the matrix has been used as an analytical tool. It also should be used to examine new creative approaches to either:

Market extension

- What additional new customer groups could be targeted for the existing offering categories provided.

Offering range extension

- What new products/services could be introduced to broaden the range provided to existing customer groups.

The 'Customer-Offering Matrix' is a powerful tool even used in isolation. Here, however, we are using it as part of a structured process. A particularly important link is to the Directional Policy Matrix discussed later in this chapter. This enables the attractiveness of each SBU to be assessed and highlights relevant options for future development.

The matrix can provide a further interesting insight into the underlying dynamics of the business of each SBU cell if the following two facts are recorded.

Level of sales (£) achieved

Profit contribution (£) generated

This highlights the profitability of the customer group across the range of offerings (as well as offering category profitability across the customer groups served). In certain organisations this will reveal a mix of attractive and unattractive relationships with a specific customer group. This may well be sensible where there is a deliberate trade-off to provide a comprehensive package to the customer. In practice it is not uncommon for certain SBUs to reveal a negative performance without any such justifying logic! Equally often a company does not have the data to identify the financial performance of specific SBUs. This reveals a deficiency in the management information available for decision taking.

SBU analysis: the benefits

Clear segmentation of any business using the customer/offering matrix seeks to avoid a bland, unfocussed approach to the market. The process enables:

Key Learning Point

- Identification of the strategically most important SBUs
- Clear definition of the specific competitors and meaningful comparison of performance
- A focused understanding of customer group needs to be developed and satisfaction tested
- Targeted differentiation strategies to be developed
- Advertising and promotional activity to be designed and delivered based on a clear understanding of the dynamics of the market
- Resource allocation and prioritisation.

Here this has been introduced as a specific 'exercise' to identify SBUs; in practice, regular on-going information flows and management decision taking needs to be focused on each individual SBU, as well as managing the overall portfolio of SBUs.

The initial process of developing the customer/offering matrix may take considerable time and effort but the process is itself productive in helping to identify what is known and highlight other areas in which vital information is lacking.

If the analysis process has been well executed it will not only have determined the right business to be in, but will also have started to prompt deliberate decisions not to be in other areas of work. This is important in clearly establishing and being able to communicate throughout the organisation:

- Those areas in which the business wishes to operate, and why
- Those areas in which the business does not wish to operate, and why.

Competitor profiling

This analysis provides for a direct ranking of the relative performance of the organisation versus that of its competitors. It should be used to take a broad view of the relative competence of the firm and the analysis must deliberately be driven from a customer perspective. It is therefore important to take into account both <u>facts</u> and <u>perceptions</u>. Customers' buying decisions are based on their perception of the relative advantages (price/cost, performance, quality etc) of the firms 'offerings' versus that of either direct competitors or substitute products/services. These perceptions may or may not correlate with the facts. Successful businesses are those that effectively manage customer perceptions to ensure that their products/services are the preferred choice.

Concept

The matrix enables a map to be developed of relative performance against each Critical Success Factor (CSF).

Key Management Concept

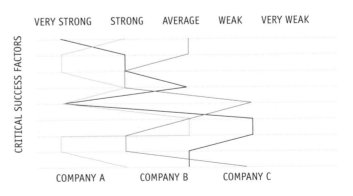

Competitor Profiling

Application

The first step is to identify the CSFs – 'What do we need to do well to win business'. These must particularly be addressed from a customer perspective. To clearly identify the CSFs it is vital that a clear definition of the market segment and customer group has been identified using the SBU analysis concept introduced in the previous section. Within any sizeable business there will be many different market segments and customer groups that are served. If too broad a definition is used the CSFs will be bland and generic, and therefore unhelpful in gaining clarity of relative performance against competitors.

The analysis relies on a sound understanding of customer perspectives and competitor performance. It will therefore draw on factual data available (from customer satisfaction surveys, market research etc) as well as the experience of managers and staff within the organisation. It also requires a clear understanding of competitor performance.

The objective of the 'profiling map' drawn is to identify gaps in relative performance. These may be:

Action Checklist

- Relative strengths which produce a source of competitive advantage. The strategic objective will be to seek to maintain this positive differentiation

- Relative weaknesses which may threaten future performance, or explain current shortfalls. The strategic objective would be to evaluate options for closing, and potentially reversing, the gap.

This visual form of analysis clearly highlights priority areas of attention to sustain and improve the performance of the business unit in the market segment.

Directional policy matrix

The purpose of the matrix is to provide a clear focus for the development priorities of the organisation. It is also sometimes referred to as the GE Grid, which was derived, when it was initially used by General Electric as a strategic analysis framework. It encourages executives to make objective decisions about each strategic business unit within the corporate portfolio, taking into account the strength of the business position and the attractiveness of the market segment in which it operates.

Concept

The matrix requires a clear analysis to be made on two determinants fundamental to business prospects:

Market segment attractiveness

- This is particularly related to the ongoing level of sector growth and profitability available.

Competitive position

- This is the strength of the position which the business currently occupies in the market/segment.

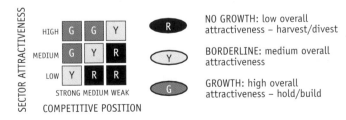

Market sector attractiveness

The analysis of Market Sector Attractiveness should reflect the following key drivers

Market factors

- Growth rate
- Volume and financial value
- Maturity
- Seasonality
- Stability

Key Management Concept

Competitive factors

- The number of competitors
- Relative size of competitors
- Intensity of competition
- Barriers to entry and exit
- Potential availability of substitute products/services
- Product lifecycles

Technology factors

- Speed of technological change
- Technology investment required
- Access to technology (patents etc)

Financial factors

- Investment funding requirement
- Working capital funding requirement
- Profit margin levels and trends
- Volatility of market

- Cost flexibility (balance of fixed and variable costs)
- Taxation policies
- Cash flow requirements

Customer factors

- Strength of customer bargaining power
- Loyalty/ability to switch
- Stability of needs and demand levels

Supplier factors

- The availability and cost of supplier inputs
- Strength of supplier bargaining power
- Strength of employee bargaining power

Social and environmental factors

- The power of pressure groups
- 'Green' acceptability of industry
- Social attitudes toward industry
- Regulatory controls and trend of legislation

Competitive position

The analysis of competitive position should reflect the following factors:

Market factors

- Market share and relative market share
- Annual growth rate of business unit sales versus competitors
- Maturity of products relative to competitors
- Quality of products/services relative to competitors
- Strength of product mix and range
- Marketing competence
- Protection of product/intellectual property (patents etc)
- Relative pricing and perceived differentiation
- Control and quality of distribution channels
- Advertising quality and responsiveness
- Level of marketing spend
- Level of customer loyalty and satisfaction

Technology factors

- Technological competence and leadership
- Quality of technology adoption and integration
- Patent protection
- Quality of manufacturing/service delivery technology

Production factors

- Costs relative to competitors
- Level of capacity utilisation

- Availability of raw materials and sub-assemblies
- Quality of inventory control
- Quality of maintenance

Organisational factors

- Quality of employees
- Effectiveness of management systems
- Culture and fit with market
- Quality of training and development
- Staff attraction and retention

Financial factors

- Financial resources available
- Access to capital
- Relative cost of capital
- Inventory and debtor management
- Relationships with suppliers

Application

The Directional Policy Matrix is an important tool for business portfolio analysis and seeks to clearly reflect the **position** and **attractiveness** of each Strategic Business Unit (SBU).

In practice the strategy for an individual SBU, within the overall corporate, must take into account its strategic importance to the overall group, synergy with other areas of activity, the ability to offer a full range of products/services to a customer etc. However, unless these wider considerations are an overriding constraint to decision taking the following table illustrates likely responses to each position:

	STRONG	MEDIUM	WEAK
HIGH	**G1** Enhance leadership Sub-segment and extend to strengthen position Invest to maintain	**G2** Seek cost effective differentiation Concentrate focus to gain position	**Y3** Aggressively pursue options for competitive advantage Prepare for retaliation Evaluate investment and risk
MEDIUM	**G2** Hold leadership position Focus on most attractive segments Use strength to suppress competition	**Y2** Seek to further clarify growth/harvest segments Avoid inertia	**R3** Consider alternative areas for development Evaluate options to sell share
LOW	**Y1** Maintain leadership in most attractive segments Use strength to re-engineer sector attractiveness Harvest less attractive segments	**R2** Consider further segmentation and focus to gain advantage Evaluate options to sell share	**R1** Sell, if possible, or close down

SECTOR ATTRACTIVENESS (vertical axis)

COMPETITIVE POSITION (horizontal axis)

Action Checklist

When applying the Directional Policy Matrix it is important to accurately define the relevant criteria for the market segment to evaluate in a logical, structured way the current competitive position. It is essential to test and challenge assumptions about relative competitive position. Often managers' perceptions are quite different to the reality and at variance with the actual views of customers (and potential customers if an improved competitive position is to be pursued).

There are two particular ways of applying the matrix :

Option one

Mapping the position of SBUs onto the matrix to examine their relative position, and that of the key competitors.

Q What is the relative position and attractiveness of the SBU?

Q How is the SBU positioned versus competitors?

Q How are these relative positions changing and for what reasons?

Option two

Applying the identified matrix positions (indicated as 'G1', 'Y3', 'R2' etc on the table) to the Customer/Offering matrix previously described. This is illustrated below for a simple business.

CUSTOMER GROUPS / OFFERINGS	A	B	C	D
1	G2	G1		R3
2	G2		Y1	
3		G2		R3
4				Y3

An offering category may have a different positioning depending on the customer group being considered. For example, in the case of a pharmaceuticals manufacturer, a certain product range may be competitively weak when considered in relation to state healthcare as a customer group, but competitively strong in the private healthcare market where differing purchase criteria may be used. Equally the private healthcare sector may itself provide significantly more market attractiveness in terms of growth and profitability.

This second option provides a powerful visualisation of the real attractiveness of offering categories and customer groups. This enables strategic issues and options to be considered. It is also a starting point for considering the correct priorities for resource use (management time, staff resource, financial investment, etc). It also highlights where continuing to operate an R1 (apparently very unattractive SBU) can be vital to integrate into an attractive range of other SBUs as part of a comprehensive package to certain customer groups.

Competitive positioning: generic strategies

Here we will consider the practical application of an approach developed by Michael Porter.

The model provides a framework for industry or market sector analysis to examine how a firm can compete effectively in order to create and sustain competitive advantage.

Concept

The concept identifies the two distinct drivers of competitive advantage :

- **Low cost** – *This is where the business manages its cost base to ensure that it is the lowest cost producer – thereby either winning a greater volume of business through lower prices than competitors can sustain and continue to be profitable, or charging comparable prices and therefore achieving a higher level of profitability.*

- **Uniqueness** – *This is where the business provides a distinct basis of differentiation (uniqueness perceived by the customer and regarded as valuable) which enables business to be won and normally a price premium attracted.*

Key Management Concept

Strategic Advantage

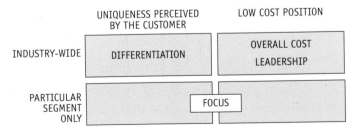

There is a further choice introduced by the model that defines the breadth of the competitive arena in which the business operates.

- **Industry wide** – *this is where the business operates across the breadth of the industry providing products/services for a wide range of customer needs. An example in the car industry would be Vauxhall with an extensive range across a broad base of customers.*

- **Particular segment only** – *in this context the business has chosen to concentrate attention on a defined segment of the market. This is called a focus strategy. An example would be BMW pursuing the luxury car segment.*

Application

The model enables us to consider the requirements of each strategy and therefore to identify action themes. The following paragraphs highlight important considerations that underlie each of the two approaches to achieving strategic advantage.

Differentiation strategy

- Identify needs and wants that are valued by the buyer

- Evaluate differentiation options and selectively add value in cost effective areas

- Establish and sustain superior performance by serving the buyer needs and wants uniquely

- Ensure that successful differentiation leads to premium prices (premium prices may reinforce perceived differentiation), or market share/volume advantages

Differentiators must maintain a broadly equivalent cost base to that of competitors to achieve above-average profitability

Differentiators must select cost effective forms of differentiation, which cannot be easily or immediately replicated or leapfrogged by competitors.

In order to pursue this strategy it is likely that the Critical Success Factors would include...

Action Checklist

...strong marketing skills

...strong co-ordination among functions

...product engineering

...amenities to attract creative people

...corporate reputation for quality

...brand strength and image

...integrated distribution channels

...quality focused incentives.

Cost leadership strategy

- Deliver a relevant quality product or service at the lowest possible cost

- Develop a significant and sustainable cost gap over the primary competitors

- Create advantage through superior management of key cost drivers

- Leading to above-average profits with industry-average prices, or market share/volume advantage.

Cost leaders must maintain an acceptable level of satisfaction of buyer needs. Cost leadership is often in conflict with differentiation i.e. to achieve differentiation adds cost thereby removing the potential cost leadership advantage.

In order to pursue this strategy it is likely that the Critical Success Factors would include...

> ...capital for investment in technology
>
> ...business process re-engineering competence
>
> ...tight cost control
>
> ...labour efficiency controls
>
> ...design for ease of manufacture/service delivery
>
> ...low cost distribution channels
>
> ...quantitative volume/cost incentives.

Focus strategy

For many more complex organisations operating in sophisticated markets an 'industry-wide' approach locks the business into the 'mindset' of differentiation or cost leadership. This may lead to inappropriate approaches being taken to certain segments of the market. Competitive positioning is best examined at Strategic Business Unit (SBU) level where the relevant competitive strategy can be identified in direct relation to specific customers and competitors. This enables a tailored approach to be adopted for each SBU. In turn this may lead to cost efficiency by ensuring that only the specific competitive requirements of the segment are addressed rather than, for example, market/industry wide differentiation approaches which may add significant cost.

Strategic direction – Common problems

The differentiation strategy is often the most 'attractive' in that it provides the opportunity for a more creative approach to the market. For this reason the organisation tends to be marketing led. It is vital in these business units that the cost/benefit analysis of any new form of differentiation is thoroughly evaluated. In addition, sensitivity analysis must be used to look at the viability of the associated cost base at different levels of sales performance and in different market conditions.

Key Learning Point

The primary challenge with differentiation is one of competitor replication, where the advantage is temporary and, once replicated, becomes an increase in the industry/market cost base for all competitors. This upward migration of the cost base can over time destroy an attractive market segment.

The cost leadership strategy often requires a 'lean' culture and is usually perceived as 'unattractive' with the consistent focus on cost management and efficiency. A tendency to be production or operations led therefore emerges. This produces a concentration on standardisation of products, components and processes with the minimisation of variations/derivatives. A fine balance needs to be achieved between maintaining a narrow range of products/services and meeting the varying needs of different customer groups.

It is these tensions between either providing a differentiated approach to match customer need and gain competitive advantage, or pursuing cost leadership to gain profit margin and value advantage, that often leads in practice to a mixed approach. This means that the advantages of neither competitive position are achieved. This being 'stuck in the middle' yields no competitive advantage and erodes the position of the business unit.

Summary... the facts of competitive life

- There are two distinct competitive positions: differentiated or low cost

- Each Strategic Business Unit (SBU) must have a clearly defined differentiated or low cost strategy

- With a differentiation strategy, effective control of the cost base to ensure effectiveness of spending remains important

- With a cost leadership strategy, maintenance of product /service adequacy and customer satisfaction remains important

- The reason for the strategy must be understood and pursued by all managers

- The chosen strategy must be superior to that of competitors and lead to competitive advantage

- No one competitive position succeeds for all market segments /SBUs.

Competitive positioning: differentiation

This model of the differentiation process, developed by Shiv Mathur provides an outstandingly powerful framework for considering alternative approaches to creating competitive advantage. It provides an insight into the processes of differentiation and competitor positioning which builds on the concepts introduced by Michael Porter's 'generic strategies' as described in the preceding pages.

Concept

Businesses seek to influence potential customers to purchase their products and services by a process of differentiation. The benefit of differentiating an offering from that of the competitor is that it encourages initial customer purchase and ongoing customer loyalty. It may also enable a price premium to be commanded. The way in which a business differentiates can be considered using a simple matrix.

Key Management Concept

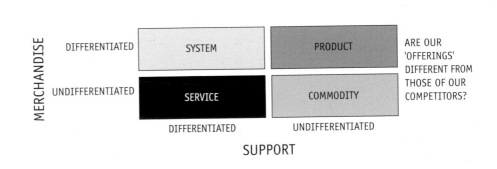

The two axes of the matrix are defined as:

Merchandise – those things, which are provided to the customer, e.g. a car service, an office refurbishment, a stereo system etc.

Support – advice, training or assistance (help in making choices, use of the merchandise etc) given to customers, e.g. knowledge of customers specific requirements and past history.

The implications of the four cells of the matrix are:

Merchandise Differentiated Support Differentiated	The firm fully analyses the customer's requirements in detail and ensures 'tailor-made' merchandise as part of a unique package. Defined as **'System'**.
Merchandise Differentiated Support Differentiated	Differentiated from the merchandise of other providers by, say, technical and physical features; branding also comes into play. No focused support provided. Defined as **'Product'**.
Merchandise Undifferentiated Support Differentiated	The firm provides a unique programme aimed at assisting the customer to assess and specify their requirements and these are subsequently supplied from a standard offering range with great expertise. Defined as **'Service'**.
Merchandise Undifferentiated Support Undifferentiated	The merchandise is sold with technical specifications and other features undifferentiated from those of competitors; nor does the firm provide differentiated support for the customer in assessing or responding to individual requirements. Defined as **'Commodity'**.

Application

This simple model enables us to consider the features of a competitive offering and to develop approaches for gaining competitive advantage. The model below uses the matrix to highlight the normal competitive processes at work in the market place.

Action Checklist

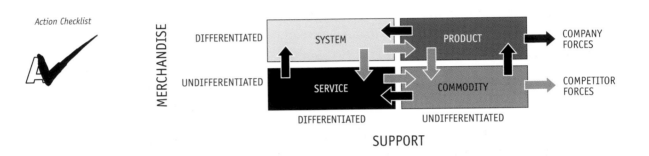

Whilst the company should be continually seeking to find new ways of differentiation, the natural competitor response is to match or preferably exceed each new increment of differentiation. This is normally a continuing process, often with different products or services holding the superior differentiated position from time to time. However, where there is no distinct advantage in the eyes of the customer the market becomes 'commodity' where the only form of differentiation is price.

The matrix should be used to consider the following four questions.

Q What is our current position within the matrix?

Q Where in the matrix are our competitors?

Q What are the existing bases of differentiation used by ourselves and our competitors?

Q What are the potential bases of differentiation which could be used by our business to gain advantage?

When using the matrix, care needs to be taken to ensure that the stated competitive positions reflect reality rather than management perception. In some markets several competitors will see themselves as being differentiated and therefore positioned in the 'system' box. If these individual forms of perceived differentiation are not valued high by the customer no real competitive advantage has been attained. The competition are therefore truly positioned in the 'commodity' box. The acid test of achieved differentiation is superior market position, volume and/or a price advantage.

Merchandise differentiation

Helpfully the Shiv Mathur approach highlights the key drivers of each of the two primary basis of differentiation. Merchandise is particularly driven by :

Content: the tangible attributes of the product or service received by the customer. For example technical capability, functions, durability etc.

Image: this is less tangible, but nevertheless valued by the customer attributes. For example brand reputation which supports product confidence (Sony) or status/exclusivity (BMW).

Again deliberate decisions need to be made concerning alternative routes to competitive advantage. There are four distinct choices of competitive position:

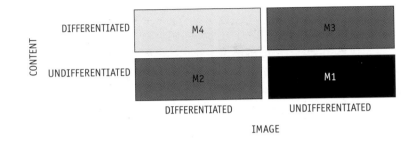

Position **M1** appropriately described as **'standard'** – there is nothing differentiated about the merchandise (product or service). For example, matches or milk.

Position **M4** is described as **'exclusive'** – where merchandise differentiation has been achieved on both axes. For example, Porsche or Intel.

Support differentiation

Again there are two key drivers:

> **Expertise:** the inherent knowledge of the product or service and its general application such as technical competence, market knowledge, experience etc.

Personalisation: the effort devoted to understanding the specific needs/ requirements/application of the customer and provision of a specifically tailored response. There are four distinct choices of competitive position:

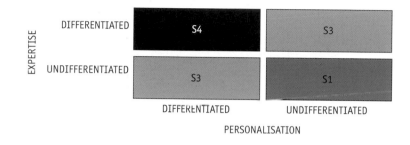

Position **S1** described as **'trader'** – indicates that there is nothing distinguishable about either the level of competence of the approach, to tailoring the offering to the circumstances of the customer. This is perhaps most easily likened to the market trader who sells primarily on price and availability. For example, petrol.

Position **S4** described as **'consultant'** is differentiated on both dimensions. For example, management consultancy or luxury bathroom design and fitting.

Differentiation and price

Differentiation and price are linked. Normally achieving differentiation enables a price premium to be charged. However, this additional price potential may be sacrificed to enable increased volume/market share to be achieved. This in itself may provide a further competitive advantage as high volume drives down unit costs.

Price is also a factor which itself influences customer perception. In certain markets/segments high price is seen as overcharging or 'taking advantage' of

Key Learning Point

the customer – naturally leading to lower price competitive offerings being chosen. However, in other markets/segments price is in itself a positive differentiator. In this case premium price reinforces the perception of premium product – in fact a lower price would damage the competitive positioning. Examples would be luxury cars or exclusive hotels where the tangible additional value provided, versus a lower profile competitor, is significantly less than the price premium attracted. The price reinforces the positive perception. Here brand image and exclusivity are directly supported by price. To reduce price would actually reduce attractiveness.

Summary – achieving competitive advantage

There are a range of potential differentiation choices driven by **Merchandise** (comprising Content and Image) and **Support** (comprising Expertise and Personalisation).

Where no real differentiation exists the business is operating as a commodity and the customer will choose on price and availability. A low cost competitive strategy will be required to support a lowest (or equal) price whilst still retaining average industry profitability.

The differentiation matrixes should be used to map the business offerings and the relative position of competitors. Based on this analysis, alternative market strategies should be examined and a choice made.

Mastering the
Volume – Cost – Profit
relationship

Chapter 4

'It's unwise to pay too much, but it's worse to pay too little.
When you pay too much, all you lose is a little money – that is all.
When you pay too little, you sometimes lose everything because the thing you bought
was incapable of doing the thing it was bought to do.
The common law of business balance prohibits paying a little
and getting a lot – it can't be done. If you deal with the lowest bidder,
it is as well to add something for the risk you run, and if you do that,
you will have enough to pay for something better.'

John Ruskin

Content

Overview		The importance of understanding the financial characteristics of the business.
The Contribution Approach	Q	Which products / services are financially attractive
	Q	Where is the salesforce most effective?
	Q	Which customers / groups are the most financially attractive?
Product and Service Pricing	Q	What is the effect of price reduction?
	Q	What is the effect of price increase?
	Q	How sensitive is profitability to volume / price changes?
Cost Profiling	Q	What is the spending on support activities?
	Q	How effective is this spending?
	Q	Where are the opportunities for improved effectiveness?

Overview

In this chapter we will consider some of the basic concepts of preparing and reviewing business financial plans. These will be the straightforward and practical 'ground rules'. Unfortunately many businesses fail to understand or apply these concepts.

Volume – Cost – Profit relationships

Directors and managers will usually focus on sales (volume and value) and profit performance. Future plans are often based on what has been achieved in the past with an emphasis on growth and, for larger businesses, increased market share. The impact on the business of a divergence from plan is not fully considered or even perhaps recognised.

The assumptions made in any plan will never be perfect and changes may occur in many areas. For example:

- Sales volumes
- Cost of materials and supplies
- Prices
- Labour costs
- Productive efficiency
- Interest rates
- Gross profit margin.

Directors and managers need to understand the **financial characteristics of the business** – how it will respond to change. To identify these financial characteristics we need to ensure that we have the right information to enable judgements to be made.

Unless the **Volume – Cost – Profit Relationships** are properly understood decisions regarding the future of the business may not produce the results expected. In the worst case they may place the future of the business at risk. Surprisingly many businessmen are unable to clearly and accurately describe the important financial dynamics of their business. For example, they have not thought through and evaluated key questions such as:

Q   Which products/services are the most attractive financially ? *or*

Q   What would be the effect of an increase/decrease in sales? *or*

Q   What would be the effect of a change in the mix of business? *or*

Q   What would be the impact of increased competition and pressure on selling prices?

This chapter will introduce a series of basic principles, which are fundamental to decision taking. The subsequent chapter *Mastering option appraisal* will further develop these concepts in the context of strategy evaluation.

The contribution approach

This chapter started by stating that we need to understand the **financial characteristics of the business** – how it will respond to change. To develop this understanding we need to identify and separate:

Variable costs – expenses which vary in direct proportion to the volume of sales activity

Fixed costs – expenses which tend to remain constant, irrespective of the level of activity (naturally within limits).

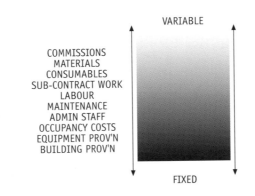

Concept

This separation will enable us to identify the **CONTRIBUTION – the margin of sales value over the variable cost of the sales** i.e. the contribution which the activity, product or service makes to the fixed costs of the business.

A well-run business will recognise the need to make the distinction between cost types and reflect this approach in their management reporting and future planning. The following is a simple illustration of the way in which the information may be presented:

For example

	Product X	Product Y	Total
Sales	**4000**	**6000**	**10000**
Variable costs			
Materials	1200	1800	3000
Direct labour	1200	2400	3600
Total	2400	4200	6600
Contribution margin	**1600**	**1800**	**3400**
Contribution margin %	**40%**	**30%**	
Fixed costs			
Management & Admin			2000
Premises costs			800
Total			2800
Profit before interest			**600**

The advantages of this approach are that:

- **Variable costs are identified with the activity, product or service**
- **Fixed costs remain unallocated – therefore not distorting the figures**
- **Contribution margin is the key focus** – this emphasises the contribution to fixed costs made by each area of activity.

Application

The first step is naturally to establish the contribution margin performance of each area of the business. It is surprising how many even sophisticated businesses lack a real understanding of the profit (contribution) generated from their various activities, products and services. Without this data, decision taking becomes less logic based and relies on intuition, and luck!

Establishment of a database of contribution information enables three important aspects of performance analysis to be undertaken:

Product/service contribution

- Identifying the achievement of each area of the business portfolio.

Sales executive contribution

- Tracking contribution generated by each sales representative/sales manager provides a superior management mechanism in comparison to sales volume or value achievement.

Customer contribution

- Using the contribution database to evaluate the performance of each customer/segment based on the range of products or services consumed.

These three dimensions provide the foundation for performance review and business planning.

Product and service pricing

In this section we examine the likely financial impact of different pricing decisions. This emphasises the importance of understanding the effect of pricing on the Real Income (Contribution Margin) and therefore overall profitability of the business.

Concept

This approach illustrates the financial effects of different pricing strategies. We will use as an example a manufacturing company producing a small range of mechanical components for heating and ventilation equipment. These are primarily used in the construction industry. There is significant competition although the company has a good reputation. The management is considering two alternative pricing strategies to improve performance.

Reducing prices

Alternative one: REDUCE PRICES BY 10% – to attract increased sales volume

	Existing performance	**Price less 10%**
Sales	200,000	180,000
Variable costs	150,000	150,000
Contribution Margin (Real Income)	50,000	30,000
Contribution Margin %	25%	16.7%

This analysis helps to identify that...

> ... real Income per £1 of sales falls from £0.25p to £0.167p

> ... without additional volume the Contribution Margin (i.e. the contribution to the fixed costs or overheads of the business) falls by £20,000. If Fixed Costs remain unchanged bottom line Profit will also fall by £20,000

> ... to achieve the existing Contribution Margin of £50,000 sales of £300,000 must be achieved. (This is determined by calculating how many contributions of £0.167p in the £1 must be produced to generate £50,000 i.e. £50,000/0.167).

Sales volume must increase from £180,000 to £300,000 – a 67% rise just to stand still!

For most companies to achieve this level of increase would require considerable effort and probably the need to incur some additional costs. We will assume that our manufacturing business requires an advertising/promotional campaign (£5,000) and an additional member for the sales team (£10,000) – what will be the effect:

Additional fixed costs	£15,000
(and therefore Contribution Margin required)	
Contribution Margin %	16.7%
Therefore further Sales required to cover costs	£90,000

Sales volume must now increase from £180,000 to £390,000 – an incredible 117% rise

Increasing prices

Alternative two: INCREASE PRICES BY 10%

	Existing performance	**Price plus 10%**
Sales	200,000	220,000
Variable Costs	150,000	150,000
Contribution Margin (Real Income)	**50,000**	**70,000**
Contribution Margin %	25%	31.8%

With this alternative we can identify that…

> … real Income per £1 of sales rises from £0.25p to £0.318p

> … without loss of volume the Contribution Margin increases by £20,000

> … to achieve the existing Contribution Margin of £50,000 sales of £157,233 must be achieved (i.e. £50,000/0.318)

> **Sales volume could fall from £200,000 to £157,233 –**
> **a fall of 28% before the company becomes worse off!**

Working capital considerations

In examining both alternatives for our manufacturing company we have concentrated on the cost – volume – profit implications. However, this has ignored the potential impact on working capital. In practice it would be necessary to also consider the following financial effects:

	Prices less 10% effect may be	Prices plus 10% effect may be
Product Volume	– need to double	– fall by one quarter
Raw Materials Stock Work–in–Progress Finished Goods Stock }	– average holding, and cash tied up, will rise	– average holding, and cash tied up, will fall
Debtors	– average outstanding and cash tied up, will rise	– average outstanding and cash tied up, will fall
Creditors	– average liability and finance used, will rise	– average liability and finance used, will fall

Here we are considering the potential additional cash tied–up (reducing prices) or cash released (increasing prices). These changes affect the cost of financing the business – the interest paid on borrowing – and therefore increases or decreases the overheads which need to be covered by the Contribution Margin.

Application

Naturally for your own business you would be able to make more accurate assessments of these working capital changes. However, even this simplified approach provides clear evidence that **Profit and Cash effects cannot be considered in isolation from each other.** This additional, or reduced, cash requirement changes again the sales target for each alternative.

From these illustrations we can see how important it is for business directors and managers to understand properly **the financial characteristics of the business**. We have seen that this requires the identification of **Volume – Cost – Profit – <u>and</u> Cash relationships**.

The following two graphs illustrate the direct impact on volume of a 10% or 20% change in prices. The behaviour of this Volume – Price linkage is dependent on the level of the Contribution Margin for the particular business. Spend a short time studying these graphs to ensure that you understand the principles **– how do pricing changes affect your business?**

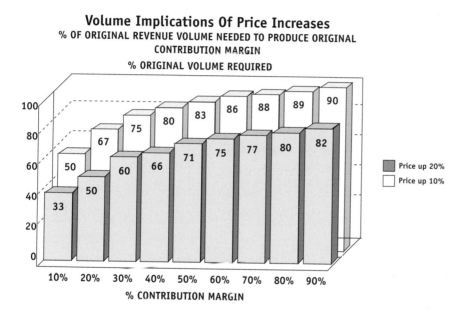

Volume Implications Of Price Increases

% OF ORIGINAL REVENUE VOLUME NEEDED TO PRODUCE ORIGINAL CONTRIBUTION MARGIN

% ORIGINAL VOLUME REQUIRED

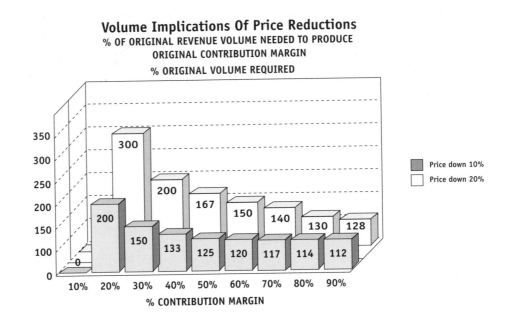

Volume Implications Of Price Reductions
% OF ORIGINAL REVENUE VOLUME NEEDED TO PRODUCE
ORIGINAL CONTRIBUTION MARGIN

The traditional 'gut' reaction to pressure to improve performance is to endeavour to boost volume, often by reducing prices and increasing sales effort. In some businesses this policy has been pursued to the extent that the total contribution margin achievable, if 100% of capacity is used and sold, is insufficient to meet the fixed costs of the business. A hopeless situation!   Actual case histories include:

- *An engineering company where company fixed costs were greater than maximum production line throughput times product contribution margin*

- *A printing business where company fixed costs were greater than maximum press capacity times average job contribution margin*

- *A ferry shipping operator where vessel fixed costs were greater than total 'certificated' passenger capacity times average contribution margin.*

In some circumstances reducing prices will be a valid approach – in other conditions increasing prices will be the correct policy. In some it will be appropriate to hold prices. **Formal, but simple, evaluation of options using the Contribution Approach will identify the Threats, and the Opportunities.**

Cost profiling

The business planning and budget setting processes used in many businesses tend to produce incremental changes in performance, often particularly achieved by small adjustments to the level of costs incurred – improving financial **efficiency**. This Cost Profiling analytical technique seeks to identify potential opportunities for more radical changes to the business cost base. It focuses on improving financial **effectiveness** by examining the relationship between costs incurred and benefits to the business.

Concept

There are two key preparatory stages in the cost profiling process.

Activity cost assessment

The on–going 'activities' of the organisation are identified; for example customer enquiry handling, preparation of weekly management reports, production engineering etc. These activities may involve many departments/business units across the organisation, thereby incurring cost in each location. Using the budgets/management accounts data for each 'cost centre' (i.e. an organisation unit where costs are incurred) an analysis is prepared to identify the costs associated with each activity. Through this process the entire costs of the business are analysed by activity.

Cost Profiling – Activity Cost

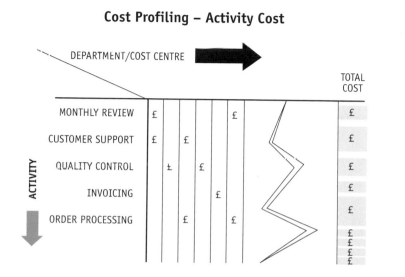

Key Management Concept

Activity benefit assessment

The focus here is to identify the 'value to the business' of the activity. The first step is to identify a set of criteria against which benefit can be judged. These criteria are the organisation's Critical Success Factors (CSFs) which derive from the strategic, market and organisational analysis discussed elsewhere in this book. Critical Success Factors are those things that the organisation needs to do well if it is to be successful.

The activities and the CSFs are entered into a second matrix. Each activity is then scored against each CSF to reflect its value to supporting that CSF. A simple scoring system may be used, say '0' ... of no value, to '10' ... fundamental to delivery of that CSF.

This ranking is normally undertaken by groups of senior executives and managers working in teams to agree the scores. The output from each group is then correlated to identify an overall response.

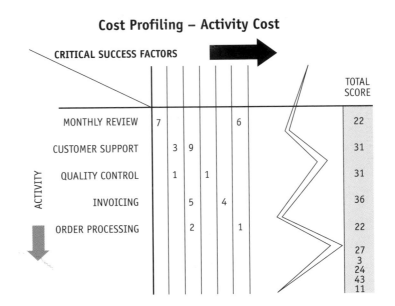

Cost Profiling – Activity Cost

ACTIVITY							TOTAL SCORE
MONTHLY REVIEW	7				6		22
CUSTOMER SUPPORT		3	9				31
QUALITY CONTROL		1		1			31
INVOICING			5		4		36
ORDER PROCESSING			2			1	22
							27
							3
							24
							43
							11

CRITICAL SUCCESS FACTORS

Application

The two sets of rankings described in the previous paragraphs – Activity/Cost and Activity/Benefit – are then brought together in a Cost/Benefit matrix. An illustrative example of this matrix is shown on the following page.

Cost Profiling – cost/benefit map

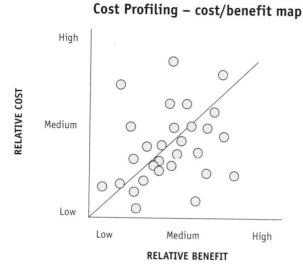

Action Checklist

The objective of the Cost Profiling technique is to identify the Cost/Benefit attributes of each activity within the organisation. The Cost/Benefit 'map' highlights this relationship and draws particular attention to those activities which fall away from what is perhaps the 'expected' relationship indicated by the diagonal line.

Where an activity is 'low cost/high benefit' it is appropriate to evaluate the additional benefit that would occur if spending was increased.

When an activity is 'high cost/low benefit' it is appropriate to evaluate the opportunities and effect of reduced spending.

The **advantages** of the approach include:

- The identification of current effective spending and ineffective spending by requiring a complete review of resourcing and cost levels
- Recognition of the specific relationship between activity and cost
- That it is challenging and establishes financial and operational goals for performance improvement.

The potential **disadvantage** is that it can be time consuming to prepare the data with the required level of accuracy. However, as part of a strategic review it is an important technique for examining the cost effectiveness of spending within the organisation.

Mastering organisational analysis

··

Chapter 5

'Organisational flexibility is essential. Rates of change have speeded up. The hierarchical organisation is slow to respond. Decisions taken at the centre are too far away from the coal face. While the centre seeks local and relevant understanding, delays in decision making result.

In today's turbulent business environment speed of decision making is critically important – decisions should be pushed down the organisation and as close to the customers as possible.'

Sir John Harvey-Jones MBE, quoted in *The Responsive Organisation*, BIM

Content

Overview   The organisation lifecycle, re-birth and
                                     harnessing the potential

McKinsey '7S' Model   Q   What is the identified strategy?
                             Q   How well is the organisation prepared to
                                     support the successful pursual of that
                                     strategy?
                             Q   What are the key areas in which change
                                     needs to be effected?

Overview – moving to a new level of success

Organisations can no longer afford to be static. The changing demands of the business environment and competitor pressure dictate at the very least regular adaption and in many cases fundamental shifts. Products have a lifecycle involving revisions, re-positioning and replacement – organisations have similar lifecycle changes but these are often far more difficult to achieve.

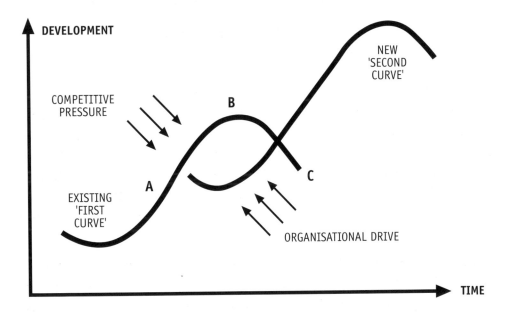

Point A is the rising success of the business as the organisation seeks and achieves superiority over its competitors. Point B is the pinnacle of success perhaps evidenced by strong market position and internal stability. The challenge is to recognise when the organisation is approaching, or at, point B and predicting when the decline toward point C will begin (and at what pace!). There are many 'triggers' which may necessitate this fundamental re-birth of the organisation, such as : economic boom or recession, a change in technology, new or intensified competition and so on.

The key issue for leaders is recognising the need for fundamental change whilst the organisation is on the ascent rather than the descent – and then taking action! When the organisation is on the descent it is often too busy fighting the 'slide' and too short of resources, particularly cash, to implement the leap to the next curve. Death may come quickly or slowly – 'failure to take action until too late' is the most common factor evidenced by research into business failure.

> *'A company is not a machine, but a living organism'*

Arie de Geus

In this context it is fascinating to reflect that most companies desire to survive, grow and prosper *but* the average life expectancy of a company is less than twenty years. The evidence is that even those organisations that achieve large multi-business/multi-national status rarely survive beyond 40 years. Only a limited number of companies buck this early to the grave trend. General Electric, Siemens, Philip Morris, Proctor & Gamble, DuPont and Mitsui are world-renowned companies that have survived, grown and prospered for over 100 years.

Arie de Geus *(The Living Company)* and James Collins/Jerry Porras *(Built to Last)* examine the traits that distinguish those longer-term 'visionary' companies from the 'also rans'. The concept of re-birth is evidenced as organisations are driven by visionary opportunities leading to fundamental shifts in organisational focus. For example, American Express which was founded in freight transportation and has re-birthed as a financial services provider.

The renowned 3M leader William McKnight moulded the organisation to embrace creativity with the 'soft' belief

'build fences around people, and you'll get sheep'

to this we should add the 'hard' fact

'build walls around an organisation, and you'll get a coffin'

Effective organisational leadership requires focus on both the 'hard' and the 'soft' issues. Often it is the 'soft' aspects that present the most significant barriers to change.

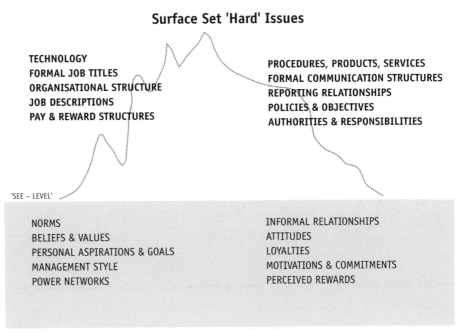

Surface Set 'Hard' Issues

TECHNOLOGY
FORMAL JOB TITLES
ORGANISATIONAL STRUCTURE
JOB DESCRIPTIONS
PAY & REWARD STRUCTURES

PROCEDURES, PRODUCTS, SERVICES
FORMAL COMMUNICATION STRUCTURES
REPORTING RELATIONSHIPS
POLICIES & OBJECTIVES
AUTHORITIES & RESPONSIBILITIES

'SEE – LEVEL'

NORMS
BELIEFS & VALUES
PERSONAL ASPIRATIONS & GOALS
MANAGEMENT STYLE
POWER NETWORKS

INFORMAL RELATIONSHIPS
ATTITUDES
LOYALTIES
MOTIVATIONS & COMMITMENTS
PERCEIVED REWARDS

DEEP SET 'SOFT' ISSUES

Driving successful evolution

A major evolutionary leap requires a tangible, visible strategy supported by clear corporate goals and a common sense of purpose. Success depends on harnessing each aspect of the organisation – the culture, the people and the systems – and focusing attention in the same direction.

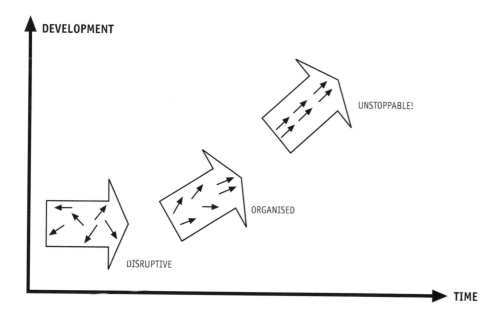

These concepts are expanded in more detail in the next section that considers how to profile the organisation using the McKinsey '7S' model.

McKinsey '7S' model

This concept which is often referred to as the McKinsey '7S' model provides a framework which is helpful to assess the readiness of the organisation for change. The original model, developed by R Pascale, and highlighted by Peters and Waterman in the 1980s text *'In Search of Excellence'* highlights ***shared values*** as at the heart of every organisation. This leans toward the 'soft' factors as the driving force. This is a logical but perhaps somewhat biased view. In practice we observe that **strategy** is (or should be!) an equally potent driving force for the organisation. We should therefore also recognise the central importance of strategy, which together with shared values set the direction for the organisation. The other five further elements then need to be focused to support the integrated strategy and shared values of the organisation.

Concept

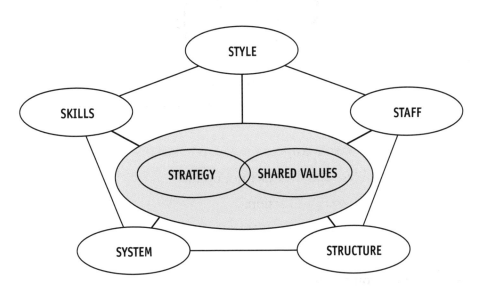

The following paragraphs provide a definition of each ellipse and highlight some typical features for success.

Strategy – This is the clear and communicated direction and goals for the organisation supported by a coherent set of actions aimed at gaining a sustainable advantage over competition. The orientation of each other factor must be evaluated and changes introduced to ensure compatibility with the strategy.

Shared values – The appropriate culture and beliefs that support the needs and environment of the business. The ideas of what are right and desirable. For example:

- Quality and customer satisfaction (Marks & Spencer)
- Competitor orientation
- Customer service (IBM)
- Innovative culture (Hewlett Packard/3M)
- Willingness to change.

Key Management Concept

Skills – The capabilities possessed by the organisation as a whole as distinct from those of individuals. Some companies perform extraordinary feats with ordinary people. For example:

- Strategic thinking ability
- Responsiveness to change
- Ability to analyse based on fact not opinion
- Ability to turn ideas into action
- Product development capability
- Entrepreneurial focus
- Marketing competence
- Production control.

Style – This also reflects aspects of culture. It is linked to the management paradigm –'the way we do things here'. For example:

- Autocratic vs democratic
- Concentration on consensus building to ensure commitment to change
- Enthusiasm
- Focus on external achievement and continuous progress
- Integrity
- 'Open' culture.

Staff – The appropriate resources to meet the demands of the existing business and future strategy. For example:

- Ability to recruit, develop and retain staff of sufficient quality
- Staff retention
- High fliers vs team players
- Quality of resources
- Old vs young
- Levels of competence
- Creative vs analytical.

Structure – The management and overall organisational structure to match the future needs. For example:

- Responsibilities and accountabilities defined
- Clear, relevant and simple
- Provides for career development and motivation of staff
- Flexible and responsive to change
- Organisational hierarchy.

Systems – These are the techniques, working procedures, computer systems, communication systems etc. They may be formal or informal 'customary practices'. The processes through which things get done on a day to day basis. For example:

- Management information systems
- Customer information systems
- Authority levels
- Manpower planning.

Activity

Application

The model should be regarded as a framework for change management. It provides a checklist of areas that need to be carefully considered and integrated to support successful strategy implementation.

The following questionnaire can be used to examine the effectiveness of each element of the organisation.

For your business you should consider each statement and indicate how true these statements are in relation to your own organisation.

Strategy	Strongly disagree	Disagree	Neither agree nor disagree	Agree	Strongly agree
1. Longer term strategy and plans are well defined	1	2	3	4	5
2. Longer term strategy and plans are effectively communicated	1	2	3	4	5
3. There is clarity throughout the business concerning the business vision and direction	1	2	3	4	5
4. The management team focuses on the medium and long term as well as short term issues	1	2	3	4	5

Structure

	Strongly disagree	Disagree	Neither agree nor disagree	Agree	Strongly agree
5. Manpower is at an optimum level	1	2	3	4	5
6. Resources are organised according to business priorities	1	2	3	4	5
7. There are the minimum of controls and management levels in the organisation	1	2	3	4	5
8. Responsibilities and accountabilities are clear	1	2	3	4	5
9. Responsibility and authority are well matched	1	2	3	4	5
10. The organisation structure is flexible and responsive to situations and changing customer needs	1	2	3	4	5
11. The organisation structure is integrated, rather than segregated and operating in isolated departments	1	2	3	4	5

Style

	Strongly disagree	Disagree	Neither agree nor disagree	Agree	Strongly agree
12. Delegation and innovation are encouraged	1	2	3	4	5
13. There is a management emphasis on helping rather than telling.	1	2	3	4	5
14. Individual and group achievements are recognised and rewarded.	1	2	3	4	5
15. Performance is measured against objective standards	1	2	3	4	5
16. Performance targets are viewed as demanding but achievable	1	2	3	4	5

	Strongly disagree	Disagree	Neither agree nor disagree	Agree	Strongly agree
Shared values					
17. There is a high level of genuine loyalty to the business	1	2	3	4	5
18. There is positive belief in the value of the products and services offered	1	2	3	4	5
19. There is a real belief in internal co-operation at all levels	1	2	3	4	5
20. People have a real commitment to continuous improvement	1	2	3	4	5
Staff					
21. People are valued as individuals and treated with respect	1	2	3	4	5
22. Peoples' abilities and potential are well understood and positively exploited	1	2	3	4	5
23. Generally high calibre people are employed	1	2	3	4	5
24. People are used for their strengths, not penalised for their weaknesses	1	2	3	4	5

	Strongly disagree	Disagree	Neither agree nor disagree	Agree	Strongly agree
Skills					
25. Skills are adequate to achieve business objectives	1	2	3	4	5
26. Skill gaps are identified and addressed	1	2	3	4	5
27. Skills are refined, improved and developed to meet changing business needs	1	2	3	4	5
28. Skills are shared and transferred within the organisation	1	2	3	4	5
Systems					
29. Planning and forecasting processes are effective	1	2	3	4	5
30. Tight controls of capital expenditure are present	1	2	3	4	5
31. Effective budget management is a priority	1	2	3	4	5
32. Stocks, debtors and cash flow are strictly controlled	1	2	3	4	5
33. There are timely and effective staff communication systems	1	2	3	4	5
34. Effective procedures for staff performance appraisal exist	1	2	3	4	5
35. Business and manpower plans are linked and integrated	1	2	3	4	5
36. There are effective systems for spotting and developing talent.	1	2	3	4	5

In practical application you will have circled a range of 'Scores' for each question. To provide an overall summary it is helpful to total the score for each of the '7S' sections and transfer this into the matrix below.

	Score given	Total available	% effectiveness
Strategy		20	
Structure		35	
Style		25	
Shared values		20	
Staff		20	
Skills		20	
Systems		40	
Overall total		180	

This analysis provides a broad overview of the organisational effectiveness of your business and focuses attention on areas where you perceive particular areas of strength or weakness.

Summary

The following is a structure to summarise the key issues and action themes arising from the '7S' analysis.

Element	Existing attributes		Changes required	Implementation	
	+ve	-ve		Action themes	Potential barriers
Strategy					
Structure					
Style					
Shared values					
Staff					
Skills					
Systems					

Existing attributes – describes the identified strengths and weaknesses that currently exist within the organisation.

Changes required - describes the changes which will be necessary to integrate each of the elements with the future strategy.

Implementation – describes the necessary actions/activities to effect the change(s) required and identify the potential barriers which could be encountered in implementation.

Mastering
option appraisal

Chapter 6

*'Before you meet a handsome prince
you have to kiss a lot of toads.'*

Content

Overview

A summary of evaluation techniques to quantify and compare alternative business development opportunities

Force-Field Analysis

Q What are the primary changes being pursued?

Q What will reinforce successful change?

Q What will constrain successful change?

Stakeholder Analysis

Q Who are the key individuals / groups affected by the change?

Q What is likely to be their impact on the potential of success?

Q Where should attention be focused to minimise risk?

Financial Sensitivity and Risk Exposure

Q What are the commercial risk factors?

Q What is the effect on profitability and cashflow?

Q What must be achieved to break-even and what margin of safety exists?

Evaluating Business Development Options

Q What evaluation approach should be used?

Q How is return calculated?

Q How are alternative options compared and choice made?

AID Analysis : Attractiveness vs Implementation Difficulty

Q What is the attractiveness of the development option?

Q What are the likely implementation difficulties?

Q What is the overall balance of risk and reward?

Overview

Option appraisal is not a straightforward process of 'running the numbers'. A series of quantitative and qualitative factors are concerned. Simplifying the process there are two key dimensions:

Attractiveness – concerned with aspects such as:

- Financial return
- Market presence
- Customer attraction.

Implementation difficulty – concerned with aspects such as :

- Commercial risk and sensitivity of figures
- Internal capabilities
- Stakeholder acceptance.

One of the essential foundations of effective Option Appraisal is to deal with facts and reality. Too often the emotional desire to pursue an 'attractive' strategy outweighs logic. This is not to say that vision, entrepreneurial drive and risk taking are wrong. These vital factors are necessary qualities in any successful organisation but they need to be supported by rational analysis. This requires evaluation of the vision, quantification of the risks and the identification of actions which can be taken to reduce the seriousness/impact of these risks. This chapter provides a series of approaches to support the structured evaluation of business development options.

Force-field analysis

This technique helps to identify those forces that support or restrict the implementation of change. These are usually described as *Driving Forces* and *Restraining Forces*.

Concept

In every change process there are Driving and Restraining forces. For positive progress to take place it is vital that the overall Driving Forces outweigh the Restraining Forces. A visual summary of the forces in an actual situation can be illustrated in a similar format to the diagram below.

Key Management Concept

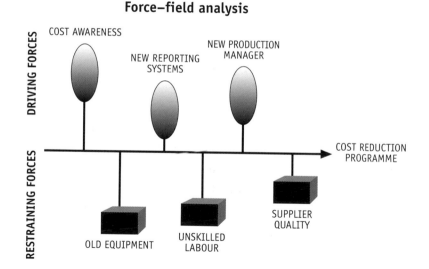

To visualise the impact of each item it is helpful to draw the length of each line to reflect the relative strengths of each force. When the forces have been identified attention is directed to implementing actions which will reduce the effect of Restraining Forces and enhance the impact of Driving Forces.

Application

The Force-Field Analysis technique can be applied to many change situations, significant and small. In simple terms the process is applied as follows:

Action Checklist

1. *Describe the planned change – the objective*

2. *List the Driving Forces that support the planned change above the centre line with vertical lines representing the probable strength of the force.*

3. *List the Restraining Forces that oppose the change below the centre line. Again use the vertical line to represent the probable strength of the force.*

4. *Consider the Restraining Forces that pose the greatest threat and agree actions to reduce / eliminate impact. Often breaking down the barriers to change will prove more effective than seeking to further promote the Driving Forces.*

5. *Consider the Driving Forces, which will provide the best impetus for change and agree actions to enhance their impact.*

Stakeholder analysis

Stakeholder Analysis is a helpful technique for considering the potential influence of various individuals or groups ('stakeholders') on the successful implementation of a proposed change.

Concept

To examine the likely impact of each stakeholder it is necessary to consider two aspects:

- Their **Attitude** – will they be supportive or unsupportive, resistant or open etc to the proposed change?

- Their **Influence** – to what degree can they exert influence due to their position/power on the change process? This influence could be either supportive or constraining depending on their attitude as described above.

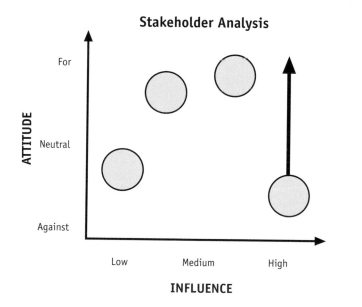

Key Management Concept

Application

Each circle on the grid represents an individual stakeholder or stakeholder group. Assessing both *attitude* and *influence* draws the focus of attention to those stakeholders that are most likely to be obstacles to success. Consideration then needs to be given to how the attitude of that individual/group can be improved, or how their influence can be reduced. Where there is a stakeholder identified as being of 'high' influence and positively 'for' the change it is important to consider how to harness this potential.

Identifying financial sensitivity and evaluating risk exposure

In this section we will further develop some of the financial planning principles introduced in the earlier chapter *'Mastering the Volume – Cost – Profit Relationship'*. This identified the financial characteristics of the business and the interaction between volume of sales achieved, fixed and variable costs and profitability.

Concept

There is no single 'right' set of relationships. The pricing and contribution margin, fixed costs, sales volumes and working capital all need to be appropriate to the operational and market conditions under which the business is operating. The following pages provide some simple approaches to analysing what is appropriate (or not appropriate!) for an individual business.

Identifying risk factors

Successful business owners and managers recognise business opportunities but balance the desire to pursue these with a realistic, and fully evaluated, view of the risks involved. They will also respond quickly to external pressures, which require that they re-assess the appropriateness of the way in which they run their business.

A summary of the Risk Factors on which they will focus is provided below. Each of the points mentioned are essential areas for consideration when business plans are prepared. However they fall into two categories:

External – Outside the direct influence of the management of the business. For example: Performance of the Economy, Stability of the Industry, Competitor Pricing, Interest Rates.

Internal – Can be directly influenced by the management of the business. For example: Pricing, level of Variable Costs, level of Fixed Costs.

Business managers need to understand the external issues and appropriately plan for and control the internal aspects.

Q How thoroughly does your business understand and evaluate in a structured way these external issues?

Q How well does your business reflect the external issues in your internal plans?

Risk factor	Area of focus
Performance of economy	• Stability of the industry
Industry sales	• Level of competition and market penetration
Market segment sales	• Competition in segment • Penetration in segment
Business sales	• Pricing and competitor pricing • Level of variable costs • 'Production' efficiency and capacity
Business contribution margin	• Level of 'fixed' costs
Business trading profit	• Gearing/borrowing • Interest rates • Level of debt repayment • Working capital funding • Capital spending
Business cash surplus or cash requirement	

Key Learning Point

Earlier in this book we considered the *Price – Volume* relationship and the use of Contribution Margin. Another important focus is the *Volume – Cost* relationship and the effect of Fixed Costs.

For a particular business situation external issues and risk factors identified in the table will dictate how stable, or unstable, demand for a given product (or service) is likely to be.

If demand is generally stable – it may be sensible for a business to carry relatively inflexible resources and therefore fixed costs – for example an engineering company purchasing all the necessary machinery and employing the labour etc, to enable all manufacturing, assembly and packing operations to be undertaken in-house. The company is therefore able to reap all of the profit benefit from the products.

If demand is generally unstable – a company may deliberately sub-contract certain volumes of work or part of the process. When demand falls their own resources remain well utilised but the level of sub-contract work is reduced. This means that a smaller proportion of total costs is fixed.

Many businesses fail because they get 'locked-in' with resources that cannot be reduced or shed as demand changes. In simple terms they do not recognise the need to link demand and resources as illustrated in the following matrix.

Key Learning Point

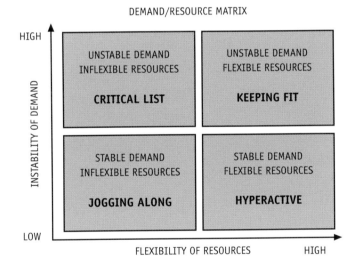

How stable is demand for your products or services?

How flexible are your resources? (i.e. variable costs vs fixed costs).

Profit vs cash

The following diagram highlights the key differences between Profit (Profit and Loss) and Cash (Funds Flow) analysis. The figures are illustrative but powerfully demonstrate the fact that the profit performance and cash performance of a business can be significantly different.

Key Learning Point

Profit Based

Cash Based

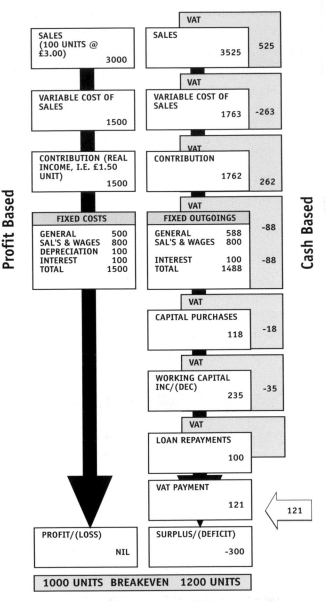

		VAT
SALES (100 UNITS @ £3.00) 3000	**SALES** 3525	525
		VAT
VARIABLE COST OF SALES 1500	**VARIABLE COST OF SALES** 1763	-263
		VAT
CONTRIBUTION (REAL INCOME, I.E. £1.50 UNIT) 1500	**CONTRIBUTION** 1762	262
		VAT
FIXED COSTS GENERAL 500 SAL'S & WAGES 800 DEPRECIATION 100 INTEREST 100 TOTAL 1500	**FIXED OUTGOINGS** GENERAL 588 SAL'S & WAGES 800 INTEREST 100 TOTAL 1488	-88 -88
		VAT
	CAPITAL PURCHASES 118	-18
		VAT
	WORKING CAPITAL INC/(DEC) 235	-35
		VAT
	LOAN REPAYMENTS 100	
	VAT PAYMENT 121	121
PROFIT/(LOSS) NIL	**SURPLUS/(DEFICIT)** -300	

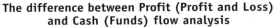

1000 UNITS BREAKEVEN 1200 UNITS

**The difference between Profit (Profit and Loss)
and Cash (Funds) flow analysis**

- The left-hand column of the diagram deals with Profit analysis. The elements are a summary of the figures that you will normally be able to identify from business management accounts, budgets or annual accounts. These sources of data will provide VAT (Value Added Tax) exclusive figures.

- The right hand column deals with Cash analysis. These figures will be available from a business cash flow summary or cash plan. The figures in the white boxes are VAT inclusive with the VAT effect shown in the shaded boxes. The total of the net VAT collected naturally ends up as a cash outpayment.

At the bottom of the diagram you will see the two Breakeven Points, Profit based and Cash based. They key issue is that Cash Breakeven requires a 20% higher sales achievement than Profit Breakeven. This is not unusual and it is important to remember that profitability ***does not guarantee solvency***. This is a vital principle when considering strategy. The evaluation of options must be based on the predicted future cash flows – simple profitability does not necessarily indicate success. This is further highlighted in the Proposal Evaluation section later in this chapter.

Cash breakeven implications

The previous paragraphs emphasise that trading performance is only one of the influences on the cash position of a business. There are three major elements in cash flow analysis:

Trading cash flow – the Profit or Loss of the business (adjusted to eliminate non-cash items, most commonly depreciation)

Working capital cash flow – changes in the funding required primarily for stocks and debtors adjusted by creditor finance used

Capital cash flow – requirements for asset purchases or repayment of previous borrowings for purchase of assets.

The following is a simplified illustration of the *Cash Breakeven* concept to demonstrate the key considerations. This simple approach can be applied to many business situations.

For example

Motofast is a small car servicing and repair business. The owner has asked their bank for a 24 months loan, with repayments at six monthly intervals, to purchase a 'service tester' for tuning and fault diagnosis. The capital sum is £28000 and interest in Year 1 will be £4700.

The business charges customers based on labour hours taken, plus parts on which there is a relatively small profit margin. In the last 12 months Motofast has sold 3740 hours.

Using some basic facts about the Motofast business, and the contribution approach that we have discussed earlier in the book we can make an evaluation of the potential effect of the new borrowing as shown below:

	£
Retail labour rate per hour	30.00
Mechanics pay per hour	10.00
Contribution margin per labour hour	**20.00** (66%)
Loan servicing in Year 1	
– capital repayment	14000
– interest	4700
	18700
Contribution margin per labour hour	20
Therefore additional sales of labour hours necessary to service the loan	**935 hrs**
Actual labour hours sold in last 12 months	3740 hrs
Therefore increase in business required	**25%**

This analysis would enable Motofast to highlight the following issues that are important considerations for the success of the proposal.

Have the implications of servicing the loan been fully considered?

Can 25% extra hours be sold?

Will an extra mechanic be required?

Is the space/tooling available for an extra mechanic?

This Cash Breakeven concept requires a focus on two key aspects:

- **The level of 'fixed outgoings'**

These are the definite cash commitments of the business, which do not vary directly with the level of business activity. Normally these will comprise the following elements and the total of 'fixed outgoings' will be calculated as shown.

'Fixed Costs' – these are the normal trading expenses which are not variable.

Less   **Depreciation** (this is usually included as a fixed cost but is not a cash item – it therefore needs to be taken out of the fixed cost figure).

Add   **Working Capital increase/(decrease)**
This will reflect the cash impact of changes in the levels of stocks, debtors and creditors

Add   **Capital Purchases**
This is required spending on new or replacement assets such as land, buildings, machinery, equipment etc.

Add   **Loan Repayments**
The required repayment of 'principal' for borrowings, e.g. loans/leases. (The interest will have been included as a 'fixed cost' in the first calculation, above, as a trading expense).

Equals **Total fixed outgoings** (fixed cash commitments)

- **The cash margin of safety**

Using the contribution margin (sales value *less* variable cost of sales) the cash breakeven point can be calculated:

$$\frac{\textbf{Total fixed outgoings}}{\textbf{Contribution margin}} = \textbf{Cash breakeven sales target}$$

The Cash Margin of Safety is the difference between planned (or actual) Sales and the Breakeven Sales target calculated. This can be expressed as a monetary figure or, more helpfully, as a percentage.

Application

The following is an example of the Cash Breakeven and Cash Margin of Safety concepts.

Example - cash breakeven

Company X is a small but rapidly expanding manufacturing business. The range of products and the normal sales mix produces a Contribution Margin of 20%.

Fixed outgoings have been forecast for the next twelve months as follows:

	£	£
Fixed costs		
	80000	
Less depreciation	5000	
		75000
Working capital		
– increase in finished goods stock	8000	
– decrease in debtors	(1000)	
– increase in creditors (due to more favourable supplier terms)	(2000)	
		5000
Capital purchases		
– new finishing machine	7000	
– packing equipment	2000	
		9000
Loan repayments		
– four quarterly repayments of principal on previous borrowing at £2000 per qtr		8000
Total 'fixed outgoings'		**97000**

The level of sales necessary to achieve **cash breakeven** can be calculated using the formula previously given i.e.

$$\frac{£97,000}{0.20} = £485,000$$

This means that sales of £485,000 will be required at an average 20% contribution margin to achieve Cash Breakeven i.e. all cash commitments could be met from cash generated by the business without the need to take any further borrowings. If sales fall below £485,000 it will be necessary to borrow monies to meet these commitments.

If the business is currently forecasting to achieve sales of £500,000 the **_Cash Margin of Safety_** would be:

$$\frac{£500,000 - £485,000}{£500,000} \times 100\% = \textbf{3.0\%}$$

This indicates that a fall in sales performance of greater than 3.0% would necessitate further borrowing – a low Margin of Safety!

Profitability and cashflow   risk responses

The following paragraphs concentrate on the three factors which we have identified, that may leave a business vulnerable in terms of profitability and cashflow. These are summarised as:

Low margin of safety

- The business will be vulnerable to a reduction in the level of sales achieved or an increase in the level of costs and cash outgoings.

Low contribution ratio

- A small contribution per unit will be vulnerable to competitive pricing action or customer price resistance. Equally an increase in variable costs or an unfavourable change in product mix will significantly affect results.

Key Management Concept

High fixed costs (or in cash terms **high 'fixed' outgoings**)

- A reduction in sales volume or pressure on the contribution margin is likely to leave fixed costs uncovered. The business will also be vulnerable to inflation in fixed costs.

Application

If performance deteriorates action must be taken to increase Real Income (Contribution Margin), reduce Fixed Costs or reduce Cash Commitments – preferably all three areas will be targeted for action. Some key points of focus are highlighted below:

Increase real income

Increase Sales Value and Market Share

- Reduce prices
- Increase advertising/promotion
- Additional sales effort/resource
- Improvements to product/service to enhance differentiation

Action Checklist

Increase contribution margin

- Increase prices
- Change product mix
- Reduce selling costs (e.g. commissions and distribution)
- Improve efficiency
- Reduce waste
- Re-negotiate supplier prices
- Reduce pay rates
- Eliminate overtime
- Review 'product engineering' (how the product is made or how the service is provided)
- Improve 'production' systems

Reduce fixed costs

Reduce level of costs

- Improve management/admin efficiency
- Eliminate management 'perks'
- Identify lower cost alternatives
  - premises
  - services
  - systems
- Reduce staffing

Turn fixed costs into variable costs

- Sub-contract activities rather than do 'in-house' and only use when required

Reduce cash commitments

Review overdraft/debt/equity structure

- Introduce equity and reduce debt

- Re-finance 'hardcore' overdraft borrowing

- Investigate alternative sources of finance

Reduce working capital requirements

- Review debtor control, payment terms and policy for granting credit

- Reduce any unnecessary stocks (including raw materials and work-In-progress where relevant)

- Extend supplier credit and re-negotiate terms where possible

Reduce capital expenditure

- Prioritise capital spending and restrict to 'essential' or 'self-financing'

- Research cheaper alternatives

  – repair of existing

  – other suppliers

  – second-hand vs new

  – rent/lease vs buy

  – contract-out work rather than do 'in-house'

Evaluating business development options

This section introduces the basic concepts for the financial appraisal and comparison of alternative business development proposals.

Concept

The purpose of evaluating business development proposals is to enable managers to:

Identify the costs and benefits of options available

Compare the differences between the individual alternatives proposed

Decide which option is most attractive and appropriate

Key Management Concept

The final decision as to which scheme(s) will be implemented will reflect the advantages and disadvantages of each option. These advantages and disadvantages will be quantified wherever possible, but in practice there will also be many qualitative factors that may bear heavily on the final decision.

A range of financial and non-financial information needs to be available for a balanced decision to be made on the implementation of significant initiatives. These initiatives will often tie-up large sums of money and set the future direction so it is important that costly mistakes are avoided.

We need to be thorough in the approach to preparing investment proposals and to identify all the relevant costs, consider the impact of risk and uncertainty and be aware how the initiative will impact on other areas of the business. The previous sections of this chapter have identified a series of approaches to option appraisal and risk assessment that will help to evaluate the 'confidence factor', which underlies the financial projections.

Principles of effective appraisal

Cash, or in particular, **cash flow,** is the focus when evaluating proposed courses of action – whether we are examining a customer contract, an asset replacement or a company acquisition.

For each project under consideration it is necessary to estimate what the likely cashflows will be over the life of the project. These can be broken into three elements.

Initial

- Comprising initial investment and any one-off set up costs

Life of scheme

- Expressed as net annual cash inflows (or outflows!) over the duration of the project

Terminal

- May include costs of disposal, scrap value or operational close down

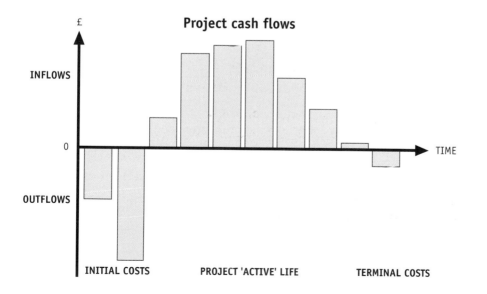

The option of **doing nothing** must be included when evaluating proposals. This will help to establish the priority of different schemes by considering the possible outcome of not going ahead. When capital resources are scarce it is particularly important to consider this option. The 'do nothing' option may be dismissed quickly, but it will also help to identify scaled down 'fall back' options stemming from the current situation.

The success of a project will be dependent on a number of factors. The following are some that will be important to consider at the evaluation stage:

- Clear understanding of business objectives
- Realistic financial projections
- Balanced evaluation of risks
- Clear areas of responsibility
- Effective project management
- Good team work
- Thorough planning
- Technical knowledge
- Commitment to make it work.

Application

There are three primary techniques commonly used for project appraisal:

- *Payback period*
- *Average rate of return*
- *Discounted cash flow*

The following paragraphs examine each of these three in turn.

Payback period method

This approach compares schemes by calculating how long it would take to payback the original investment from profits (positive cashflows) earned. We can examine how this works by using a simple example:

Carest Ltd runs nursing homes for the elderly. The company is considering building a small extension on one of its three existing sites. The life of the premises will be 40 years in each case, but with different site conditions and local variations in staff pay and charging policies. The projected net cashflows for the alternative schemes are shown in the table. The total of the net cash flows over the structural life, years 1-40, is also shown

Year	Inview	Lakeside	Valley
	£000	£000	£000
0	-200	-250	-150
1	50	50	25
2	50	100	50
3	50	**100**	**75**
4	**50**	100	75
5+	50	100	75
Total 1-40	**2000**	**3950**	**2925**

We can see that there is a net outflow of cash (shown as a minus figure) where the initial investment is made. Traditionally this initial investment period is referred to as 'year 0'. In years 1-5 the net inflow of cash, or surplus, is shown. In our example the payback period for each scheme is indicated in italic. In the case of Inview it takes four years with an inflow of £50K per year to recover the initial outlay of £200K. (Lakeside three years and Valley three years).

Average rate of return method

The average (annual) Rate of Return Method evaluates projects by comparing the return on the original sum invested. This is expressed as a percentage. Using the previous example, based on the assumed 40-year life, the results would be as follows:

Year	Inview	Lakeside	Valley
	£000	£000	£000
Initial Investment	-200	-250	-150
Cash Inflows over life years 1-40	2000	3950	2925
Net Inflow	1800	3700	2775
Average Annual Inflow (Net Inflow/40)	45.0	92.5	69.4
Average Rate of Return (Average Inflow/Initial Investment (%))	22.5	37.0	46.3

In our example we can now see that the average Rate of Return indicates Valley as the most advantageous project. Lakeside, which had been equal first under the payback period method, is significantly less attractive.

We can summarise the advantages and disadvantages of the two methods we have now illustrated as:

Payback period

+ Simple

+ Indicates risk period

- Ignores profitability

Average rate of return

+ Simple

+ Indicates profitability

- Ignores timing of net benefits

One of the main disadvantages of both methods is that neither reflects what is referred to as the time value of money i.e. when the money is received. The following paragraphs examine the Discounted Cash Flow method of evaluating schemes. This enables us to take into account the time value of money.

Discounted cash flow

When we are dealing with cash, £1 received today is more valuable than £1 received in one year's time. For example, today's £1 could be placed on deposit and earn interest during the year. In fact £0.92 invested today at 10% would be worth £1 in a year's time. Therefore, the *Present Value* of £1 received in a year's time, assuming an interest rate of 10%, is £0.91.

This approach of examining cash flows and reflecting the 'time value' of money is called *Discounted Cash Flow*.

There are two ways in which this discounted cash flow concept is commonly used.

Net present value method

- The present values for all future cash flows are evaluated at a given rate (discount rate). The rate is normally the minimum acceptable rate of return laid down as a policy guideline by the company. The sum of all the positive and negative (usually initial outlay) discounted values is the Net Present Value. If it is positive it has met the rate of return criteria (i.e. the rate of return exceeds the discount rate which has been used to 'test' the proposal).

Yield method

- A slightly more refined approach using discounted cash flows is to find the discount rate at which the sum of all the positive and negative discounted values is zero. This rate is the **Internal Rate of Return** produced by that proposal.

This internal rate of return is the compound interest rate at which the capital outlay would need to be invested to yield the same return as provided by the project being considered.

If the example of building a small extension for Carest Ltd is re-visited, we can introduce the concept of comparing all the costs on a common basis by recognising the time value, and see what difference it makes. For simplicity years 6-40 in each option are shown as one set of figures. A required rate of return ('test discount rate') of 20% has been used.

Discounted cash flow summary

Year		Inview		Lakeside		Valley	
(£000)	Discount Factor (20%)	Cash Flow	Present Value	Cash Flow	Present Value	Cash Flow	Present Value
0	1.00	-200	-200.0	-250	-250.0	-150	-150.0
1	0.83	50	41.5	50	41.5	25	20.8
2	0.69	50	34.5	100	69.0	50	34.5
3	0.57	50	28.5	100	57.0	75	42.8
4	0.48	50	24.0	100	48.0	75	36.0
5	0.40	50	20.0	100	40.0	75	30.0
6-40	1.86	50	93.0	100	186.0	75	139.5
Total (Net Present Value)			**41.5**		**191.5**		**153.5**

The table shows that the choice has changed now we have taken into account both the profitability of the schemes and the timing of the cash flows. The results of the three evaluation methods can be summarised in the following ranking table.

	Inview	Lakeside	Valley
Payback Period	3	1	1
Average Rate of Return	3	2	1
Discounted cash flow	3	1	2

Summary

The key principles of proposal financial evaluation are:

- Evaluate proposals and compare options based on cash flows
- Use Discounted Cash Flow (DCF) to take into account the time value of money
- Aim to maximise the Internal Rate of Return (IRR)
- Recognise that the absolute minimum Internal Rate of Return is the company's cost of capital.

'AID' analysis

This summary analytical tool seeks to integrate the various approaches introduced in this chapter *Mastering Option Appraisal*. It was initially developed by Tony Grundy and makes the vital link between ***Attractiveness*** and ***Implementation Difficulty*** ('AID')

Concept

The Attractiveness/Implementation Difficulty matrix is drawn as illustrated:

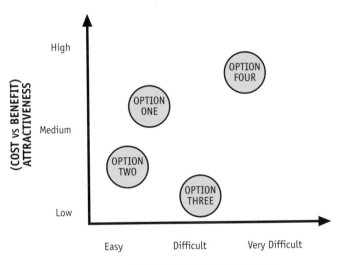

Key Management Concept

Factors that influence ***Attractiveness*** will include

- Profitability/return
- Market share
- Customer retention

- Integration with overall business
- Image/profile features.

Attractiveness therefore needs to be evaluated from a number of the perspectives highlighted earlier in this book. Financial attractiveness is obviously a primary consideration and this can be evaluated as described in the previous sections covering Evaluating Business Development Options and Financial Sensitivity and Risk Exposure.

Factors that influence ***Implementation Difficulty*** will include:

- Availability of resources
- Level of resistance from staff/management
- Skill and competence levels
- Technical complexity
- Customer resistance.

The evaluation of Implementation Difficulty is particularly linked to the Force-Field Analysis and Stakeholder Analysis techniques covered earlier in this chapter.

Application

In many cases the most attractive business development options present the greatest difficulty for successful implementation. This model seeks to emphasise that dilemma and therefore to heighten awareness of the risks involved. A careful assessment of implementation difficulty will lead to specific actions being taken to reduce the risk or, in certain cases, discarding of the option perhaps in favour of a slightly less attractive proposal with a much greater chance of success.

Action Checklist

Mastering strategic leadership

Chapter 7

*'The flame of competition has changed from smokey yellow
to intense white heat. For companies to survive and prosper
they will have to have a vision, a mission and strategy.
They will pursue the action arising from that strategy
with entrepeneurial skill and total dedication and commitment to win.'*

Peter B Ellwood,
Chief Executive
TSB Group

Content

Overview

Quality of leadership is the distinguishing factor that unites high performing businesses. It is the InSight *(\'in – sit\n: the power or act of seeing into a situation: understanding, penetrating; also intuition; source : Merridion-Webster Dictionary),* of these leaders that drives the success of these organisations.

Leadership style undoubtedly varies – Richard Branson with Virgin, Bill Gates with Microsoft, Bernd Pischetsrieder with BMW. Different styles, different industries, constant success. However, experience and research reveals that there are common factors that underpin successful executive leadership. The four key factors form a model of leadership excellence.

Strategic perspective

- The means through which the leader demonstrates visionary leadership and defines the direction of the organisation.

Market focus

- The means through which the leader shapes and drives the superior positioning of the business versus its competitors, and implements a total customer satisfaction ethos.

Results orientation

- The means through which the leader recognises business long term and short term objectives and focuses the management team and individual effort on these key deliverables.

Harnessing potential

- The means through which the leader determines priorities and directs personal and management team activities using inspirational leadership and empowerment.

The concept of mission

Mission... Strategy... Vision three related words but often used very loosely and quite differently by a range of corporations. They are terms that are found in many management textbooks. The objective here is to provide a set of definitions that are helpful in clarifying this area of Mission.

Key Management Concept

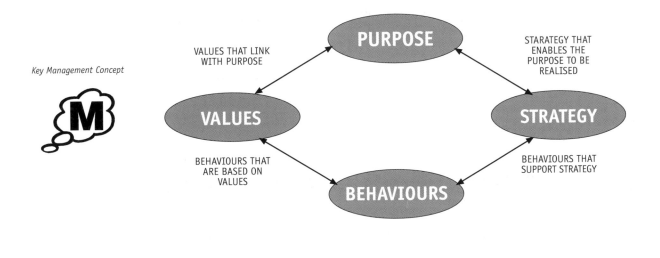

Purpose

This defines why the organisation exists. It describes the intended relationship between the corporate and the primary stakeholders (customers, shareholders, employees, suppliers'etc).

- To improve our customers' lives at home and at work by providing innovative, attractive and easy–to–use products, software and services

- To increase our shareholders' value by meeting or exceeding our profit and investment goals

- To make working at Philips an enjoyable, stimulating and challenging experience

- To conduct our business ethically and with respect for our customers, employees, shareholders, suppliers and the communities in which we operate.

Philips

To be the most respected and admired service organisation in the country.

BMW (GB)

Values

This defines the beliefs of the corporate and its leaders. These values are the foundation of the organisation ethics, its relationships (shareholders/customers employees etc) and style.

1. Delight customers

2. Value people as our greatest resource

3. Achieve quality and excellence in all actions

4. Achieve premium return on equity

5. Encourage entrepeneurial behaviour at all levels.

Philips

> Grit and gumption are preferable to inertia and intellect.
>
> Avoid the belief that dealing is preferable to working.
>
> The Victorian work ethic is not an antique.
>
> *BBA Group*

Behaviour

This defines standards or 'norms' that are expected of all involved with the organisation. These are practical principles that support the Purpose and the Values of the corporate. They become a framework for acceptance or non – acceptance.

> 'Management by wandering around'
>
> To have a well managed operation it is essential that the managers/supervisors be aware of what is happening in their areas – not just at their immediate level, but also at several levels below that.
>
> Our people are our most important resource and managers have direct responsibility for their training, their performance, and for their well-being. To do this, managers must get around to find out how their people feel about their jobs and what they feel will make their work more productive and more meaningful.
>
> *Hewlett-Packard*

Strategy

This defines the context or arena in which the corporate wishes to operate. It will often also provide a guideline on the basis on which the organisation will compete.

'Our strategy is to expand our core business globally by creating marketing alliances where beneficial or, if there is a sufficient return on capital, by investing in other airlines.'

'Competition will increase in many markets and success will depend on our ability to keep costs firmly under control.'

'To maintain a pace of quality, innovation and service delivery which keeps us ahead of the competition'.

British Airways

'We shall concentrate on markets where:

- The products are in a state of maturity or decline (Sunset Industries)
- The capital cost of market entry is high
- Fragmentation of ownership on the supply side facilitates rapid earnings growth by acquisition of contribution flows.

'Our tactic is to become dominant in our market niches by outproducing the competition, creating niches and buying competitors, and to increase profit margins by drastic cost reduction.

'We believe that the cheapest producer will win.'

BAA Group

Summary – the implications of mission

The four aspects of Mission fall into two categories:

'Soft' – the Values and Behaviour elements are those which should mould the culture or shared values aspects of the organisation.

Key Learning Point

'Hard' – the Purpose and Strategy elements are those which should set the direction of the organisation. These provide the deliverables against which business plans and their results can be judged.

To promote continued progress and success the corporate must manage both the 'soft' and the 'hard' aspects to ensure that the four elements of Mission Purpose, Values, Behaviour and Strategy – are:

- Clearly defined
- Understood throughout the organisation
- Used as a guideline for planning and decision taking
- Vigorously pursued.

Key questions

Activity

Q   What is the Purpose of your organisation?

Q   What are the Values that are relevant to the Purpose?

Q   What is the required Strategy to enable the Purpose to be realised?

Q   What are the desired behaviours that:
  – reflect the values of the organisation?
  – support the strategy being pursued?

Q   Are these four areas of Mission clearly stated?

Q   Are they fully communicated and understood?

Q   Do they provide a *living* framework for planning, review and decision taking?

Leadership: situational responsiveness

This model of leadership is a useful framework for examining which leadership styles to use in managing a team. It focuses on ideas that were developed through Hersey and Blanchard's Situational Leadership Model. Implementing the actions resulting from a strategic review and business planning process requires effective leadership. The practical framework identified alternative approaches that can be adopted to increase effectiveness in differing situations.

Concept

Hersey and Blanchard identify two major factors that affect an individual's response to your leadership :

- The emphasis you place on the **task** being carried out. The more you stress the task the more directive your behaviour will be. In other words the more likely you are to specify what you want, when you want it done by, and the way in which it should be completed.

- The emphasis you place on your **relationship** with staff. The more you stress this factor, the more supportive your leadership behaviour will be. You will encourage and praise achievement and seek to develop close relationships.

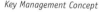

Key Management Concept

The interaction between these two factors can be shown in the form of a matrix comprising four different styles.

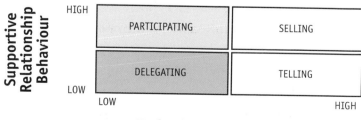

The following paragraphs describe the key leadership behaviours that reflect each of these four styles.

| Telling style | – high task – low relationship

The leader who uses this style effectively controls the work of staff closely and acts quickly to correct and redirect shortfalls in performance. They make sure staff are clear about what they have to do. They will also emphasise the use of standard procedures and stress the importance of targets and deadlines.

| Selling style | – high task – high relationship

The leader who uses this style effectively shows concern for the task as well as staff relationships. They spend time in friendly conversation, but make sure staff are clear about their responsibilities and the required standards of performance. They incorporate staff recommendations into decisions they make, and will work with a team to solve problems, but retain overall control.

| Participating style | – low task – high relationship

The leader who uses this style effectively lets staff organise and manage their own work. They do not lead them in any particular direction but allow individuals to set their own goals. They also encourage and support positive contributions. They will be available for discussion and advice, but will not push this involvement.

| Delegating style | – low task – low relationship

The leader who uses this style effectively lets staff define problems and find solutions by themselves. They avoid conflict by leaving issues alone and do not apply pressure. They do not intervene with subordinates, and deliberately take no definite action.

Application

The approach of a leader is likely to reflect a mixture of the above styles. However, individuals often have a preferred style(s) or 'natural behaviour'. The key question is which style is best, not what style does a leader use. In practice there is no such thing as 'best' style, only the 'appropriate' style in the situation.

Action Checklist

The Situational Leadership model helps us to recognise that the effective leader changes style to reflect the member of staff and the task they are working on   In relation to the individual member of staff there are two aspects to take into account:

- **Ability** – to what degree is the individual Able to do the work
- **Motivation** – to what degree is the individual Willing and Confident to do the work.

The effective leader automatically considers the member of staff as well as the task in order to decide the most appropriate leadership style to use.

Telling style

Where individuals have low competence and low motivation an effective leader will provide close supervision. For example, with new staff it is essential that close attention is paid to clarifying role, responsibilities and limits of decision taking. Attempts to use participating or selling styles are less effective because, whilst good relationships may be established, staff need to have a clear indication of their tasks and what is expected of them.

Selling style

As staff competence increases the effective leader encourages this by becoming more supportive. If they continue to be totally directive, staff would become resentful and demoralised, and perhaps unwilling to assume or take on responsibility. Equally, the participating style could fail because staff are not yet competent to make their own decisions.

Participating style

As staff become increasingly competent and motivated, an effective leader no longer needs to emphasise the importance of the task and can, instead, concentrate on establishing close productive relationships. These relationships enable the leader to keep in touch with the work. A prime benefit for the leader in moving into a participating or delegating style is that they are far less personally time consuming. Thus they should release the manager to do other work.

Delegating style

When a high level of staff competence and motivation is achieved the effective leader can withdraw, thereby providing further motivation by delegating responsibility.

Leadership style is a complex and difficult area. Few managers get it right. The situational leadership approach provides a straightforward way of assessing individuals and situations and deciding the style that is most likely to be successful. The description here has described the concept in generic leadership terms. However, in practice, it is the lack of proper leadership, applied to both the task and the people requirements, that leads to ineffective implementation of the actions arising from the strategic review and business planning processes. The strategy is fine, it is the implementation that fails.

Strategic leadership

If you are involved in leading strategic change, consider the following approach.

For each of the key players involved in the change implementation, use these steps to identify what is likely to be the most effective leadership style.

Activity

1. *Identify the most important managers or team members.*

2. *Identify the key strategy implementation tasks associated with each individual.*

3. *Evaluate their competence on the four 'ability' and 'motivation' dimensions.*

4. *Consider the most relevant leadership style to adopt – and use it!*

Name:	Key Tasks					
Role:						
Score the individual for each key task, on the four criteria below, using the following scale:						
Insufficient = 1						
Reasonable = 2						
Good = 3						
Excellent = 4						
Ability: Knowledge						
Ability: Skills						
Motivation: Confidence						
Motivation: Willingness						
Effective Style						

Mastering
performance measurement

Chapter 8

*'One thing is clear. Even if you're on the right track
you'll get run over if you just sit there.'*

Sir Allan Sheppard

Content

Overview		A summary of the different areas of focus for performance measurement.
Strategic Key Performance Indicators (SKPIs)	Q	What are the key drivers of commercial success?
	Q	What are the objectives and how is progress measured?
	Q	What are the targets and what initiatives should be pursued to achieve them?
Financial Key Performance Indicators (FKPIs)	Q	How financially attractive is the business?
	Q	How well are the financial resources managed?
	Q	How secure/solvent is the business?
Operational Key Performance Indicators (OKPIs)	Q	What are the primary areas of operational focus?
	Q	How are these integrated with the corporate Strategic Key Performance Indicators?
	Q	What are the management processes to control and motivate - achievement?
City Key Performance Indicators (CKPIs)	Q	What are the primary areas of 'city' attention?
	Q	How is corporate performance measured?
	Q	How is shareholder return measured?
Value Added	Q	Why is the concept of value added important?
	Q	How is it measured?
	Q	How does it apply in labour intensive businesses?

Overview

There are many approaches to performance management. In this chapter we will highlight some of the key principles which help to provide for a structured and balanced approach. It will cover those concepts which support the processes of management within the business as well as certain aspects related to how those outside the corporate view overall performance.

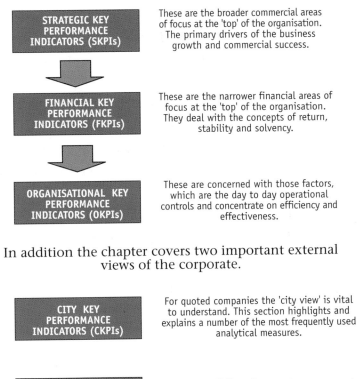

STRATEGIC KEY PERFORMANCE INDICATORS (SKPIs)	These are the broader commercial areas of focus at the 'top' of the organisation. The primary drivers of the business growth and commercial success.
FINANCIAL KEY PERFORMANCE INDICATORS (FKPIs)	These are the narrower financial areas of focus at the 'top' of the organisation. They deal with the concepts of return, stability and solvency.
ORGANISATIONAL KEY PERFORMANCE INDICATORS (OKPIs)	These are concerned with those factors, which are the day to day operational controls and concentrate on efficiency and effectiveness.

In addition the chapter covers two important external views of the corporate.

CITY KEY PERFORMANCE INDICATORS (CKPIs)	For quoted companies the 'city view' is vital to understand. This section highlights and explains a number of the most frequently used analytical measures.
VALUE ADDED	The responsibility of corporate management is to ensure that the organisation is 'creating value'. This section summarises three core approaches.

Strategic Key Performance Indicators (SKPIs)

This performance management technique highlights those factors that are critical to maintaining the strategic direction of a business. They are the foundations for ensuring a 'culture' of continuous performance improvement and preparing the overall business for both the boom and recessionary periods which typify the economic cycles in which corporates operate.

Concept

The approach is derived from a concept called 'Balanced Scorecard', which was developed by Robert Kaplan and David Norton. It reflects the following core principles:

Key Management Concept

- No single measure can provide a clear performance target or focus attention on all the critical areas of the business.

- The Balanced Scorecard seeks to minimise the common problem of information overload on business leaders by limiting the number of measures used.

- The approach is a way to clarify, simplify and then operationalise the Mission (Purpose/Values/Behaviours/Strategy) at the top of the organisation.

The Balanced Scorecard is a measurement framework and concentrates attention on the four primary perspectives of corporate performance. Each perspective focuses on a particular question fundamental to the future prosperity of the overall business.

The Balanced Scorecard

FINAL PERSPECTIVE ...how do we look to our owners?	CUSTOMER PERSPECTIVE ...how do our customers see us?
BUSINESS DEVELOPMENT PERSPECTIVE ...how can we further develop?	INTERNAL PERSPECTIVE ...what must we excel at?

Application

The following sections highlight, for each of the four dimensions of the Balanced Scorecard, a range of suggested business objectives and related Strategic Key Performance Indicators (SKPI's) i.e. the measures which are used to track progress.

Business objective	SKPI
Financial perspective –	*how do we look to our owners?*
Profitability	Net Profit Margin (%)
	Return on Total Funds (%)
Shareholder Income	Dividend Level (£)
	Dividend Cover (times)
Growth	Sales Trend (year on year growth)
Stability	Gearing (Debt: Equity) Ratio
	Interest Cover (times)

Customer perspective –	*how do our customers see us?*
Customer Care	Customer Satisfaction
Quality	Number of Complaints (No) Goodwill Spend (£)
Availability	Product/Service lead time (No. of days/weeks)
Brand Values	Management daily quality/presentation audit (No. of failures)

Business development perspective –	*how can we further develop?*
Innovation/Creativity	Overall Sales per Head (£) Unit Sales per Sales Executive (Units)
Effectiveness	Sales/Prospect ratio (%) Market Penetration (%) Customer Retention i.e. repeat business (%)
Investment	Capital Spend (£) Profit Retained in Business (% of total Net Profit)

Internal perspective –	*what must we excel at?*
Staff Retention	Staff Turnover Rate (%pa)
Personal Development	Training Days (No)
Performance	Appraisal (performance improvement trend Assessment/Development Centre Feedback
Commitment	Sickness/Absence Levels (No. of days)
Communication	Full Staff Team meetings/workshops (No)

For each of the Business Objectives the Strategic Key Performance Indicator (SKPI) represents the measurement tool. Related to each SKPI a stretching but achievable target level of performance should be set and clearly communicated to all relevant staff. To achieve this target, specific initiatives need to be identified, implemented and reviewed. This link between objectives, SKPIs, targets and initiatives is illustrated below.

The Balanced Scorecard therefore drives performance throughout the organisation. There is a direct line of integration between the Vision of the organisation and the Strategy that is being pursued. It also provides the top level 'scoring' mechanism to ensure each aspect of the business is 'on-track'.

The Balanced Scorecard Approach

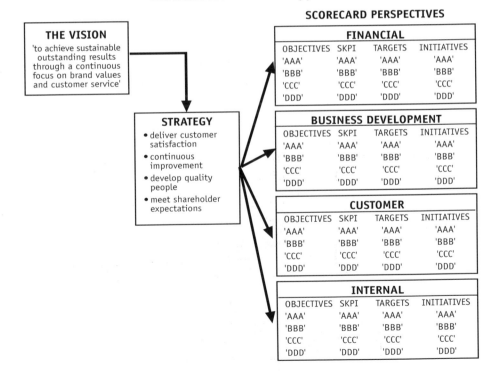

Financial Key Performance Indicators (FKPIs)

The CAP™ Approach

This technique of financial analysis is intended to provide an overview of the financial performance of the corporate. The financial ratios can be applied to the business to examine current achievement and trends. They can also be applied to competitors to enable external 'benchmarks' of performance to be established.

There are many potential ratios available but these comprise those that would be regarded as a 'core set' designed to provide an overall insight into the business and the challenges facing management. They reflect the typical approaches used by corporate management, business analysts and bankers.

Concept

Financial performance profiling recognises that there are three distinct aspects of financial performance – **Cash, Assets and Profit** *(the CAP™ Approach)*. These are summarised visually as:

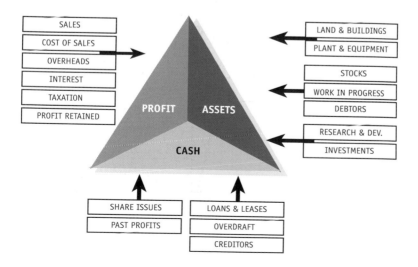

Key Management Concept

In simple terms a business is a process of investing cash in assets which in operational use make a profit.

Cash – is the money injected into the business and may come from past profits, bank loans, new shares issued to owners, etc.

Assets – for the business may, depending on the type of operation, include premises, equipment, stocks, work-in-progress, debtor's etc.

Profit – will come from sales of any of the range of business offerings.

Application

To examine the performance of the business, and its competitors, the assessment ratios highlighted in the following paragraphs are applied. The narrative provides a definition of the ratio plus brief guidance notes to support interpretation. The ratios are focused on three fundamental questions:

Q **Profit Generation** – *how good is the business at generating profits? - margin and cost management*

Q **Cash Control** – *how well is the business able to meets its commitments? – solvency and security*

Q **Asset Utilisation** – *how well does the business utilise its assets? – operational efficiency*

Profit generation

Gross Profit Margin (%) $\dfrac{\text{Gross Profit}}{\text{Turnover (Sales)}} \times 100 \ (\%)$

- Shows the gross profit as a proportion of sales
- Indicates the average contribution that a sale makes to overhead expenses
- Will be significantly affected by product mix/pricing changes

- Gross profit is after charging the direct cost of sale but does not normally include other sales related expenses such as selling expenses, delivery etc.

- Can be related to break-even analysis – what level of gross profit contribution is required to cover all 'fixed' overhead expenses.

Net Profit Margin (%) $\dfrac{\text{Net Profit (before interest)}}{\text{Turnover (Sales)}} \times 100 \, (\%)$

- Shows net margin before financing charges (normally interest), tax and non-trading expenses

- States average level of 'Bottom Line' profit achieved on sales

- Indicates degree to which overall profit levels can absorb pressure on selling prices or cost inflation.

The level of Net Profit Margin will need to be sufficient to ensure that borrowing can be serviced (interest and repayments of principal), re-investment can take place for the development of the business and equity shareholders can receive a satisfactory return. The level of Net Profit margin (% will vary considerably between industries – for example Net Margin may vary from as low as say 2-3% in construction to 25-30% with certain hi-tech products).

Return on Funds $\dfrac{\text{Net Profit (before interest)}}{\text{Net Assets}} \times 100 \, (\%)$
Employed ROFE (%)

- Shows the return on total financial resources employed in the business

- Does not take into account the sources of finance (debt vs equity) or the cost of servicing that borrowing (interest)

- Focus is on the performance of the management team in earning profit from the effective utilisation of the total capital tied up in the company

- Indicates if an adequate return is being made in comparison to

  - alternative opportunities

  - the business risk

The level of ROFE will need to be greater than the cost of funds to the business. Different sectors will produce different levels of ROFE performance depending on the attractiveness of the market and the capital intensity of the business. Achievement will normally be judged by comparison to similar businesses in the same sector.

Return on Shareholders $\underline{\text{Net Profit (before tax)}}$ X 100 (%)
Funds ROSF (%)   Shareholders Funds

- The ratio is calculated based on Net Profit after interest but normally before tax. (This is calculated after deduction of interest because this is the 'return' to the lenders)

- Reveals the level of return achieved on the total money invested by shareholders (shares paid and retained profits).

- Does not reflect the return on the realisable value of the shares (the market price) or the actual price paid for the shares if purchased on the stock market.

The level of ROSF needs to offer an attractive margin above a secure money investment to reflect the potential risk of investing in that particular type of business.

Cash control

Current Ratio   Current Assets

Current Liabilities

- Current Assets is the total of stocks + work-in-progress + debtors + cash
- Current Liabilities is the total of trade creditors + short term borrowing + overdraft + taxation liability etc.
- Shows short term asset cover for short term liabilities
- Compares value of items expected to be turned into cash with liabilities which are payable
- If ratio is < 1 business <u>may</u> have a cash flow deficiency problem
- A basic measure of likely ability to pay bills
- Assumes that stocks can be sold and that debtors are realisable.

This ratio should normally be > 1. However, it should not be too high as this may indicate poor utilisation of the working capital tied-up in trading (i.e. Stocks, WIP and Debtors).

Liquid Ratio   Debtors + Cash

(Acid or Quick Ratio)   Current Liabilities

- Shows cash and near cash cover for current liabilities
- Indicates the level of liabilities that can be met out of funds which should be securely available to the business i.e. cash and invoices outstanding (debtors).

Often this ratio will be in the range of 0.5 to 0.8 but will be sector dependent. The difference between the values of the current and liquid ratios is stock.

Interest Cover $\dfrac{\text{Net Profit (before Interest \& Tax)}}{\text{Interest}}$

- Shows number of times interest payments are covered by the level of profit achieved

- Indicates ability of business to meet interest payments

- If market conditions are unstable a low interest cover predicts possibility of not being able to service loans.

If the interest is covered <1 times this indicates that the business may need to borrow further monies simply to meet the interest payments on past borrowings – bad news! A level of 3-4 times covered would normally be considered relatively secure.

Debt : Equity Ratio $\dfrac{\text{Debt}}{\text{Equity}}$
(Gearing)

- Debt is all interest bearing funds

- Equity is the total shareholders funds (the same as Net Worth)

- Establishes the relationship between borrowed monies and shareholders funds

- Indicates how a business has been funded

- A high ratio of Debt (all loans and leases etc) indicates that:

    - lenders are bearing some of the company risk

    - dividends to shareholders may be restricted due to need to service the high level of debt interest repayment.

Note: Debt should take into account both long and short term borrowing i.e. loans, finance leases, overdrafts and other finance facilities etc. plus 'off balance sheet finance' such as operating leases, rentals and hire purchase.

- The ratio is now more commonly expressed as a percentage.

Bankers and Investors will typically look for a 1:1 (100%) ratio not to be exceeded i.e. they will lend £1 for every £1 of owners, money invested in the business. When the general economy is strong a gearing of 2:1 or 3:1 may be considered acceptable for certain businesses.

Asset utilisation

Stock Index $\dfrac{\text{Stocks}}{\text{Cost of Goods Sold}} \times 365$ ('days')
(Stock Turn)

- Shows the average number of days stock is held and therefore how often stock is turned over in a year

- Indicates control and utilisation of stocks

- Influenced by sales/stock level/stocking policies/market conditions/ stock availability requirements

- True value of stock may be significantly influenced by;

  - suppliers 'Reservation of Title' clauses (where supplier has legal title until full payment is made)

  - obsolete stocks

  - valuation and write-down policies.

This ratio will vary considerably between industries.

Debtor Index $\dfrac{\text{Trade Debtors}}{\text{Turnover (Sales)}}$ x 365 ('days')
(Debt Turn)

- An indicator of the average number of days taken to collect monies receivable

- Indicates actual terms of trade being achieved and credit control effectiveness

- May raise concerns regarding the quality of debtors:

    - included in accounts prior to work completion

    - items in dispute

    - solvency of the customers

    - customer credit vetting practices

    - effectiveness of contracting procedures.

- When interpreting remember that business turnover will include both cash sales and credit sales, this will influence the overall average calculated.

A useful indicator of overall trends which will be specifically monitored internally by debtor category/customer.

Creditor Index $\underline{\text{Creditors}}$ X 365 ('days')

(Creditor Turn)   Cost of Purchases

- Shows average number of days taken to pay bills

- Focus is on company's use (or abuse) of supplier finance

- Concerns may include –

    – full inclusion of all liabilities

    – continuity of supply

    – supplier power/influence over the business

- Cost of Goods Sold is sometimes used as a substitute for Cost of Purchases. This significantly reduces the accuracy of the index calculated.

A useful indicator of the average level of credit available to the business.

Sales/Net Assets $\underline{\text{Turnover (Sales)}}$

(Asset Utilisation)   Net Assets

- Indicates utilisation of assets i.e. value of £s earned per £1 of net asset in a trading period

- Can be significantly affected by the accuracy of the book valuation of fixed assets, particularly land and buildings.

Measures the effectiveness with which the Net Assets invested in the business are used to generate sales income. The trend of achievement should be monitored as well as comparison to other similar businesses.

Summary - building up the picture

The analytical ratios can individually be helpful in the review of past performance, future projections or competitor comparison. In addition there are several vital linkages that should be recognised to further enhance understanding and insight.

- **Return – the key drivers**

As the achievement of return is one of the paramount goals the constituent elements should be examined as:

Margin (%)		Utilisation (£)		Return (%)
$\dfrac{\text{Profit before interest}}{\text{Sales}}$	X	$\dfrac{\text{Sales}}{\text{Net Assets}}$	=	$\dfrac{\text{Profit before interest}}{\text{Net Assets}}$

Differing industry sectors will achieve an acceptable level of Return by a significantly different balance between Margin and Utilisation. An illustrative example from three leading companies would be:

	Margin (%)	X	Utilisation (£)	=	Return (%)
Construction Sector	3.1	X	5.63	=	17.4
Food Supermarkets	5.5	X	3.81	=	20.9
Engineering	9.3	X	1.90	=	17.7

The level of return is all in broadly the same range. The way in which it has been achieved is quite different, reflecting the specific characteristics of the three industry sectors. The capital-intensive engineering business must achieve a strong margin to offset the low utilisation. Conversely the low margins available in the construction sector are necessarily offset by a philosophy of low capital tie-up and 'making the assets work for you.

- **Liquidity – ability to pay**

Current Ratio $\qquad \dfrac{\text{Current Assets}}{\text{Current Liabilities}}$ (say 1.4)

Liquid Ratio $\qquad \dfrac{\text{Cash + Debtors}}{\text{Current Liabilities}}$ (say 0.6)

The difference between the values of the Current and Liquid ratios is stock i.e. the difference of 0.8 (1.4 – 0.6) is the proportion of stock to current liabilities. This means that of the current liabilities 0.6 (or 60%) are covered by fairly secure cash inflow (debtors and cash). The remaining 0.4 (or 40%) of liabilities are covered by stock.

- **Funding and security**

Interest Cover (times) $\qquad \dfrac{\text{Profit before Interest}}{\text{Interest}}$ (say 7.0)

Gearing (%) $\qquad \dfrac{\text{Debt}}{\text{Equity}}$ (say 160%)

Here the gearing in itself is high at 160%. Gearing is a risk measure. The higher the ratio the greater proportion of total finance in the business has been taken from lenders rather than shareholders' funds – i.e. equity – either through retention of profits or new share issues.

The risk consideration is that if the business hits a difficult trading period (change in market/exchange rate fluctuation/economic recession etc) repayment of outstanding principal and interest will still be required on the debt (loans, leases, hire purchase etc). The advantage of equity is that in the lean times dividend payments could cease. The higher the relationship of debt to equity the greater the underlying risk in the business.

A primary concern therefore is the ability to service the debt. Interest cover indicates how many times the interest burden is covered by profitability. The higher the 'cover' the greater the margin of safety if trading becomes difficult.

The two ratios must be read together. A high gearing of 160% may be a risk factor <u>but</u> when linked with a strong interest cover of 7.0 times it becomes much more acceptable.

- **Working capital – managing the operational 'financing gap'**

This is examining the flow of money tied-up in the day to day operations of the business, commonly referred to as 'working capital'. This may be illustrated using our three example companies as:

	Construction Sector	Food Supermarkets	Engineering
Stock Index (days)	44[1]	19	26
Debtor Index (days)	89	8[2]	64
	133	27	90
less			
Creditor Index (days)	76	65	67
Financing Gap (days)	57	(38)	23

[1] Work in progress
[2] Effect of credit cards

The most attractive by far is the Food Supermarket where a favourable gap of 38 days is evidenced i.e. the actual cash from sales is received over one month before the supplier is paid. At the other end of the spectrum is the construction business where the combined effect of cash tied-up in work in progress (stock) and extended debtor collection cannot be offset by the period taken to pay sub-contractors and suppliers. This results in an unfavourable gap of 54 days during which the business is required to finance the creditor payments.

Key Management Concept

Operational Key Performance Indicators (OKPIs)

This approach provides a framework for managing performance at operational level.

Concept

Throughout the organisation there needs to be a focus on both external performance (how the customer is satisfied) and internal performance. Customers are generally concerned with three aspects:

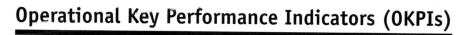

From an internal perspective the primary driver of performance and success is widely acknowledged to be the competence and commitment of the workforce at all levels. Employees are generally concerned with two aspects:

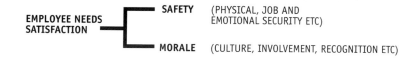

It is these five aspects of Quality, Cost, Delivery, Safety and Morale (QCDSM) that are the key areas of attention for operational performance review. In any organisation it is important to concentrate on effectiveness throughout all areas. 'Output' effectiveness is the direct result of effectiveness on each of the areas of 'Input' i.e. to achieve a high level of customer needs satisfaction, the internal processes must be focused on the concept of total (internal and external) customer satisfaction. This links with the internal customer concept where each team takes full responsibility for their output being as near as possible to 100% acceptable to the next team in the organisational process.

Effectiveness and impact

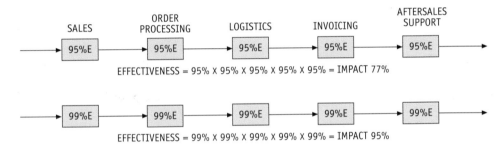

Although 95% Effectiveness appears in itself to be reasonable, the cumulative effect of this across the organisational process is a wholly unacceptable Impact of 77% achievement from a customer perspective. Concentration on performance management in each of the five QCDSM aspects is therefore vital for each team.

The QCDSM approach reflects the operational interpretation of the 'balanced scorecard' concept introduced earlier in this chapter *(Strategic Key Performance Indicators, SKPIs)*. Each team should have a scorecard reflecting these five areas of performance. Illustrative areas in which team objectives/measures would be set, are shown in the table opposite.

QCDSM Objective	Measure

Sales and Marketing

Quality	Prospect: sales, ratio number of customer claims, customer satisfaction survey results
Cost	Marketing spend/enquiries rate, sales support, spend and expense levels
Delivery	Sales volume, market share, enquiry response time, forecasting accuracy
Safety	Number of accidents, number of safety suggestions
Morale	Attendance, sickness, number of discipline incidents, staff turnover, number of suggestions, culture climate questionnaire results

Research and Development

Quality	Product reliability, manufacturability, serviceability, return factor, number of engineering changes, market acceptance
Cost	Expense levels, new product development time/cost
Delivery	Number of new products, patents, forecasting accuracy
Safety	Number of accidents, number of safety suggestions
Morale	Attendance, sickness, number of discipline incidents, staff turnover, number of suggestions, culture climate questionnaire results

Operations

Quality	Downtime, number of customer claims, defect rate, rectification level
Cost	Productivity, expenses, overtime
Delivery	On time delivery, production lead time, inventory level, availability
Safety	Number of accidents, number of safety suggestions
Morale	Attendance, sickness, number of discipline incidents, staff turnover, number of suggestions, culture climate questionnaire results

Finance

Quality	Number of errors in billing, accuracy of financial reporting, level of internal audit failures
Cost	Productivity (throughput), cost levels
Delivery	Report timeliness invoicing efficiency, creditors index (days), debtor index (days)
Safety	Number of accidents, number of safety suggestions
Morale	Attendance, sickness, number of discipline incidents, staff turnover, number of suggestions, culture climate questionnaire results

Monitoring and controlling

In most organisations there are performance review processes regularly applied (weekly sales team review/monthly management meetings etc) – the real effectiveness of these varies, as many will have experienced! However, the underlying performance management process is the same.

The PDA Cycle

The period taken to go through the cycle varies according to the organisation, the team and the task. Typically the cycle may be hourly, daily, weekly, monthly, quarterly or even annually. Hourly may be for example, toilet checking in a restaurant; yearly may be organisational culture survey.

Frequently it is the <u>Check</u> and <u>Act</u> stages that fall down.

To be effective the PDCA cycle needs to be applied to the five aspects of QCDSM. For each aspect the review cycle requires:

		Example
Objectives	A clear statement of what is desired	*Customer satisfaction*
Measures	Agreement of the measurement mechanism	*Satisfaction survey score*
Targets	The 'standard' level of achievement required	*96% Target*

The Check process then uses these clear statements as a basis for assessment of results. Based on the achieved actuals, say a score of 91%, the Act process means actually doing something to improve on-going performance. In the example it could be tele-sales staff training in relationship handling.

The PDCA cycle is a vital performance management process – in many organisations not well applied. The key questions are:

Q What are the primary PDCA cycles in our business?

Q Are these fully understood by all involved?

Q Is everyone committed to the disciplines of Check and Act?

Q Do the PDCA cycles fully reflect the needs of the business, its customers and its employees?

Q Is the review process based on clear and logical Objectives, Measures and Targets?

Q Is PDCA applied to all the operational 'balanced scorecard' areas of QCDSM?

City Key Performance Indicators (CKPIs)

This section summarises some of the most common financial analysis ratios that are used as a basis for describing company performance from an 'investor' perspective.

Return on Equity

The ROE measure is calculated as :

ROE is **Profit after Interest and Tax (PAIT)**   x   **100%**
              Equity

this is made up of	PAIT	x	Sales	x	Net Assets
	Sales		Net Assets		Equity
which is	Net Margin	x	Asset Utilisation	x	Financing Policy

- Identifies the achieved return on the shareholders investment in the business

- Reveals return based on the shareholders actual investment made (shares issued and retained profits) but does not reflect the current realisable value of that investment i.e. the market value of the shares.

Market: Book ratio

This is calculated as:

$$\frac{\textbf{Market Capitalisation}}{\textbf{Book Value (Net Worth)}}$$

Key Learning Point

- Compares the 'market value' of the business, based on the current share price, to the net balance sheet value
- Market Capitalisation is current share price x number of shares issued
- Book Value is the net balance sheet value (Net Worth) calculated as Fixed Assets + Current Assets – Current Liabilities – Long Term liabilities.

Price/Earnings ratio

This is calculated as:

$$\frac{\textbf{Market Price per Share}}{\textbf{Earnings per Share}}$$

- The P/E Ratio is probably one of the most quoted ratios by financial markets and 'city' institutions
- Earnings Per Share is profit after tax divided by the number of issued shares
- A high P/E Ratio may indicate market confidence in the company
- It is interesting to note that a P/E of say 15.0 indicates that price is fifteen times earnings. This means that on the current price the 'return' achieved is 1/15 (reverse the ratio) or about 6-7%. Naturally this 'return' would be unattractive therefore the high price reflects a market belief that future earnings will grow.

Earnings Per Share

The Earnings Per Share (EPS) is quoted by each company in their Annual Accounts. It is calculated as:

$$\frac{\textbf{Profit after Tax} \text{ (before extraordinary items)}}{\textbf{Number of Ordinary Shares}}$$

- Reveals the profit, derived from normal business operations, attributable to each ordinary share

- Normally used to examine the trend of individual company performance or to compare with other similar businesses

- Does not reveal the level of dividend actually paid but indicates the profit available for either dividend payment, or re-investment into the business. The re-investment of retained profits should in theory improve the future value of the company and consequently the share value. The shareholder therefore receives a return in two ways – dividends received and growth in share value.

Dividend Yield

This is calculated as:

$$\frac{\textbf{Dividend per Share} \times \textbf{100/75}}{\textbf{Market Price per Share}}$$

- Indicates the level of direct dividend return on shareholder investment using the existing market value of the share

- The 100/75 calculation would be used to 'gross-up' the dividend assuming a tax credit at a 25% standard tax rate. This calculation is adjusted to reflect changes in tax rate.

Dividend Cover

This is calculated as :

$$\frac{\text{Earnings per Share}}{\text{Dividend per Share}}$$

- Shows the number of times that the dividend declared could have been paid out of the current year's earnings (profits)

- Also indicates the relative proportion of profit retained in the business to finance investment

- The dividend can be greater than the earnings (profits) in the year leading to a cover of less than one. This is because dividends can be paid out of prior years retained profits.

- May indicate the degree to which *either* satisfying shareholder expectations *or* meeting the investment needs of the business are the key priority for management.

Value added

This section provides a brief overview of three increasingly used concepts of 'Value Added'. Each of these focuses on the primary business goal of creating value.

Economic Value Added (EVA)

'the measure of total factor productivity'

Peter Drucker

This is a management tool that seeks to link all decisions with the aim of maximising shareholder wealth. It integrates the four ways in which wealth can be created in a business:

- Cutting costs
- Investing in value adding initiatives
- Releasing capital from under-performing areas of activity
- Reducing the cost of capital.

Key Learning Point

EVA = Net after tax Income – Cost of Capital

Net after tax Income is Profit before Interest minus taxation

Cost of Capital is the average debt and equity rate applied to the average capital employed. The average capital employed is calculated as:

Total Assets (excl. investments and intangibles)

less Current Liabilities (excluding all overdrafts, short-term loans, leases etc)

- A positive EVA indicates that the business has created value in the year, and therefore proactively increased shareholder wealth
- A negative EVA indicates that the business has destroyed wealth

- EVA performance should be evaluated by comparing

  - the year on year trend of the company

  - industry sector performance with company performance.

Market Value Added (MVA)

This concept is increasingly used in conjunction with EVA previously discussed. It tracks the year on year growth in the value of the business to investors. The focus is again on identifying whether the company has created or destroyed value for its shareholders.

The basic calculation is:

MVA = Market Valuation of Company – Total Investment in Company

Market Valuation is the total of the current value of the company shares plus the value of all debts outstanding

Total Investment is the total of all funds raised by the business which *is the sum of :* money raised through share issues, plus retained earnings, plus total borrowings.

The calculation identifies the total market value added (wealth created) since the business was formed.

- A positive MVA indicates that the company has created value over its lifetime

- A negative MVA indicates wealth destruction

- MVA performance should be evaluated by examining the year on year trend of MVA valuations.

EVA and MVA - linking the concepts

Both EVA and MVA are useful individually for current and trend performance appraisal. Used together the two viewpoints are complementary:

- *EVA concentrates on* <u>operational wealth creation</u> *in the year*

- *MVA concentrates on the* <u>long–term wealth</u> *creation in the market (city).*

Employee Value Added (EVA)

This focuses on the value created for the business by employees, a further concept called value added.

Employee Value Added is =   **<u>Total Added Value generated by Business</u>**
Total Cost of Employees

Where Added Value is Sales <u>less</u> Cost of Purchases

- Reveals the Added Value created for each £1 of employee pay

- Should be compared to similar businesses operating in the same sector or trend within the business

- Particularly relevant for 'labour intensive' businesses.

(Note : Cost of Purchases can be estimated as total costs, excluding interest and tax, less employee costs and depreciation. Where the concept is applied as an internal performance measure Cost of Purchases is more accurately defined as the direct 'inputs' to the products of services or the business i.e. purchased materials, components, sub-contract services etc).

Mastering
new business development

Chapter 9

*'Wherever anything's being done,
it's being done by a monomaniac with a mission.'*

Peter Drucker

Content

Key Stages in Business Development

Q   What is the normal process of business development?

Q   What are the characteristics associated with each stage

Q   Where is the business now in the development process?

Key stages in business development

This section will examine the process of development of a new business or a new business unit within a corporate. The framework identifies the typical challenges and features of different stages in business development. It is important to recognise and prepare for these stages before initiating a new enterprise. It is also helpful in diagnosing where an already established business is in the process of development.

Concept

The framework identifies six key stages in the development of a business. These are:

- Pre-start-up
- Existence
- Survival
- Success
- Take-off
- Maturity.

They are shown diagrammatically on the next page.

Although the framework illustrates the development process it is not true that all ventures will progress through all six stages. Some of course will fail! However, many others may, for a long period of time, 'stick' at a stage before moving on or, in some cases, regressing to the previous stage.

Whichever stage of development the business has reached, one important driver of success will be the enthusiasm and commitment of the business leaders. There are certain qualities that are recognised as characteristics of a successful business leader there are:

- *Initiative* – being a self-starter and able to take decisions

- *Determination and persistence*

- *Resilience* – able to cope with setbacks and to work at resolving them

- *Responsiveness* – able to see the business from the outside and to adapt the product or service, if necessary, to meet the existing and changing needs of the customer

- *Influencing skills* – to gain the commitment of others.

Key Stages in Business Development

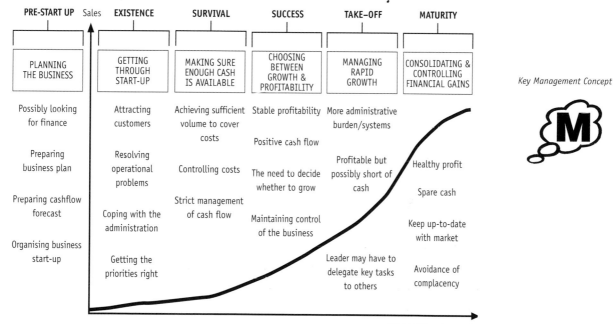

PRE-START UP	Sales	EXISTENCE	SURVIVAL	SUCCESS	TAKE–OFF	MATURITY
PLANNING THE BUSINESS		GETTING THROUGH START-UP	MAKING SURE ENOUGH CASH IS AVAILABLE	CHOOSING BETWEEN GROWTH & PROFITABILITY	MANAGING RAPID GROWTH	CONSOLIDATING & CONTROLLING FINANCIAL GAINS

Possibly looking for finance

Preparing business plan

Preparing cashflow forecast

Organising business start-up

Attracting customers

Resolving operational problems

Coping with the administration

Getting the priorities right

Achieving sufficient volume to cover costs

Controlling costs

Strict management of cash flow

Stable profitability

Positive cash flow

The need to decide whether to grow

Maintaining control of the business

More administrative burden/systems

Profitable but possibly short of cash

Leader may have to delegate key tasks to others

Healthy profit

Spare cash

Keep up-to-date with market

Avoidance of complacency

Stage of Development

Key Management Concept

{M}

Stage 1:	Pre-start-up

This is the period of planning and the identification of sources of finance. It requires a thorough assessment of the viability of the proposal. Particularly important are cash flow projections and 'what-if' analysis to examine the sensitivity/risk of the business.

Key areas to be considered will include:

Q How will the business attract and retain customers?

Q How long will the business have to wait for payment from customers?

Q How will appropriate suppliers be identified?

Q What credit terms can be established with suppliers?

Q Who are the primary competitors?

Q How intense is the competition?

Q How easily can customers be enticed away from competitors? What is the level of customer/company loyalty?

Q Is the market growing? (this makes it easier to win customers)

Q What capital investment/set up costs will be incurred?

Q What sales will be generated and what operating costs will be incurred (profitability)?

Q What receipts and payments will occur (cash flow)?

Q What would be the effect of changes in circumstances (sales volume, price, costs etc)?

Stage 2:   Existence

This stage involves a great deal of hard work. The business leader(s) may have to cope with the various managerial and commercial aspects of running the business themselves. Issues prominent at this stage often include the following:

Q   Starting the work

Q   Ensuring the prompt delivery of materials sub-assemblies or contracted in services from suppliers

Q   Maintaining schedules

Q   Meeting promised customer deadlines

Q   Achieving administration effectiveness

Q   Recruiting, training and managing staff

Q   Setting priorities for the effective use of time.

At this stage the business is likely to be cash flow vulnerable. Payment to suppliers may be required prior to delivery, and goods or services provided by the business may not be paid for until 30, 60, or 90 days after delivery. In addition many suppliers will not be willing to provide credit facilities to new start-up businesses. This puts a strain on cashflow, which can be further affected if, as is likely, things do not go to plan. The business may not necessarily be in trouble but the cash flow forecast and business plan will need to be updated to reflect changes.

Stage 3:   Survival

The business has now demonstrated that it is a practical enterprise. It has attracted customers and, at least to some degree, satisfied them with its products/services. This is when the business is generally short of cash and may not yet be showing a consistent strong profit. There are many reasons for this situation including:

- **Late or delayed payment by customers.** Frequently businesses do not give sufficient consideration to the payment details when negotiating contracts and find that customers do not pay when expected.

- **Difficulty in getting new customers.** There may be a competitive reaction from other businesses or there might be unwillingness by potential customers to try the new business.

- **Greater outgoings than expected in relation to incomings.** This can be the result of promises to buy from the business not being kept or the business being slower than expected to achieve its anticipated volume of sales/orders.

The key problem for the business at this stage is:

- **To achieve a sufficient volume of business to reach the break-even point, that is, to cover the fixed outgoings of running the business.**

Often this takes longer to achieve than planned and, therefore, puts pressure on the cash resources of the business. Again it is vital that the business plan and cashflow forecast are regularly updated so that progress can be monitored. Many businesses remain at the Survival stage for some considerable time as they struggle to achieve success and secure viability.

Stage 4:   **Success**

This is what all new business ventures aim to achieve and is normally reached after much hard work and sometimes periods of concern over survival.

To reach this stage of development, the business will have:

- **Established a loyal customer base.** This ensures that the business is able to cover its regular costs and to utilise resources well.

- **Established basic systems** for handling orders, production, and delivery, thereby providing the service efficiently.

- **Dealt with initial problems associated with the product or service.** These could have been production, product or service orientated difficulties, such as teething problems with technology, encountered in the beginning. The business will now be able to provide a consistent level of quality of service or product.

- **Reached the stage of being sure of a regular income** to meet outgoings and, probably, to have a cash surplus.

At this stage there are several new questions to be addressed

Q   How can the momentum of the business be maintained?

Q   How can surplus profits/cash flow be most effectively re-invested?

Q   Should the business be continued at the established relatively small size?

Q   Is there leadership ambition and market potential to drive the business through the next 'Take-off' stage?

Stage 5:   Take-off

The challenges at this stage are how to achieve rapid growth and how to finance it. The decision as to whether or not to enter this stage and pursue rapid growth may be influenced by the business leader wanting to make more money, desiring to lead a large business or perhaps for the status. Alternatively it could be driven by the demands of the customers who may want to put more trade with the business and who might take their trade elsewhere if the business cannot respond.

The decision to expand involves the acceptance of some risk and the need to face up to a number of issues:

- The availability of resources and good staff
- The delegation of responsibility to a wider team of managers
- The development of more specialist management skills
- The reduced day to day direct influence of the leader
- The possibility of taking on too much work as the business grows
- The danger that existing suppliers may not be able to keep up with the demands of the business.

As the business begins to expand, the typical characteristics of this stage are that the business is profitable, but it is short of cash as a result of the financing demands of the expansion (stock and debtor finance, capital investments, promotional costs, research and development etc).

Cost control will be an essential focus as detailed control often suffers due to the pace of growth and attention being diverted by operational 'crises'.

Stage 6:   Maturity

A mature business will often display the characteristics of a healthy profit and spare cash. As the enterprise moves into this stage it will be important to consolidate and control the financial surpluses achieved.

The major issues a business is likely to encounter at this stage are:

- Retaining the advantages that were evident when the business was smaller, in particular close working relationships, flexibility and entrepreneurial enthusiasm

- Avoidance of large 'corporate overhead' being established as a result of the business formalising and 'professionalising' its management systems

- Avoidance of stagnation due to lack of innovation, complacency or even arrogance, and becoming risk averse

- Identification of new opportunities and threats:

  - Growing new market segments/niches

  - Changing customer requirements

  - New competition

  - Related diversification.

Individual businesses will take different lengths of time to reach and to go through each of these six stages of development. In practice it is possible for a business to revert to one of the previous stages of development.

Application

For a new business initiative it is essential to recognise the development stages through which the enterprise is likely to pass, and prepare for the issues and challenges which will be faced.

Key Learning Point

For an established business it is helpful to identify the stage of development that the business has reached and recognise that it is a point in the development process. Decisions can then be taken to remain at that stage (if relevant) or seek to move on.

For a business unit within a corporate it is important to recognise that the same development process applies – often with the same challenges! However, these challenges are sometimes eased by the protection of an established corporate parent able to soften the impact of negative cash flow and poor profitability at the relevant stages.

The following paragraphs summarise a series of key questions which need to be addressed by the leader/owner at the outset of new business development. Whilst these are focused on a new stand-alone enterprise many are equally relevant to a new start-up business unit within a corporate.

Managerial issues

Issues relating to management of the business might include:

Q *What business experience do you have?*

- What background experience do you have relevant to this particular business?

    - How will decisions be made on a day-to-day basis? To what extent will the business rely upon your abilities?

Q *How do you intend to organise the business?*

Q *What are your long-term goals and ambitions for the business?*

Q *What plans will you make for your eventual move out of the business?*

General administration

Issues relating to the general administration of the business might include :

Q How do you plan to deal with all the administration involved in running your business?

Q How are you going to prioritise the tasks involved in running the business?

Personal freedom

Issues relating to personal freedom might include:

Q How do you think the business will affect the use of your own time?

Taking on employees

Issues relating to taking on employees might include:

Q What are you looking for in your employees?

– What labour does the business need? How skilled or unskilled does the labour need to be? How easily will you be able to find suitable labour locally? How many employees do you think you will need?

Q How well will you be able to manage your (extra) employees?

Q How will the business cope with additional labour costs?

Q How are you going to attract/retain the labour?

Q To what extent have you examined the responsibilities you will have towards employees, such as National Insurance Contributions, Health and Safety etc?

Legal and regulatory requirements

Issues relating to legal and regulatory requirements might include:

Q What legal requirements affect the running of your business?

Q To what extent have you looked at the legal requirements of running a business from home or from business premises?

Q To what extent have you considered your legal position regarding liability for business debt?

Q How will Government regulations affect your particular business?

– What do you understand about the Health and Safety at Work Act? What measures do you take/are you taking to comply with the Health and Safety at Work Act? What do you understand about your responsibilities towards employees?

Q What do you understand by product or service liability?

Q What insurance cover have you taken out to protect yourself against public/product/employer liability?

Taxation

Issues relating to taxation might include:

Q What are the tax implications of running your own business?

Q To what extent do you understand the different taxes that relate to your business?

Q What do you understand about the taxation differences between the different types of business?

Q What consideration have you given to business expenses and VAT?

Cash management

Issues relating to cash management might include:

Q What are the assumptions behind your business plan and cash flow forecast?

Q What level of bad debts do you expect?

Q How long have you assumed your customers will take to pay you?

Q How have you arrived at your assessment of the amount of finance required?

Q How have you worked out the level of sales you will need to achieve in order to break even?

Commercial issues

Customers

Issues relating to customers might include:

Q Who are your customers?

Q Where is your market?

   – What are the features of your market? What entry barriers exist for other businesses?

Q How do you plan to attract and retain your customers?

   – What is your marketing plan? How are you going to sell your product/service?

   – How are you going to advertise the product/service?

Q To what extent are your prices set by you or by your customers?

   – Who holds the power in the market – is it a 'buyers' or 'sellers' market?

Q How do you check whether your customer's expectations have been met?

Q How long do you have to wait for payment from your customers?

Q What credit terms are available to customers?

Q What are the opportunities for growth?

Suppliers

Issues relating to suppliers might include:

Q How are you going to set about finding the right suppliers?

Q Who are the main suppliers to your business?

Q What credit terms are you negotiating with suppliers?

Q To what extent are the materials you need readily available, or are special orders necessary which take time to be prepared/delivered?

Q How will a delay in supplies or an increase in prices affect your business?

  – How dependent upon them are you? How dependent upon you are your suppliers for business?

Competitors

Issues relating to competitors might include:

Q Who are your main competitors?

Q What customer loyalty do you have?

Q How easily can customers be enticed away from the competition?

Q What marketing approach do your competitors use?

Q What is the level of competition and how close is it?

Q How do their products or services compare with yours?

Q How do/will customers differentiate between your business and your competitors?

Product or service

Issues relating to the product(s) or service(s) might include:

Q What knowledge of the product/service do you have?

Q What product(s) or service(s) do you/are you going to produce?

– How appropriate are they to this market?/How are you going to cost the product(s) or service(s)?/What price will you sell at?/What will your product mix be?/Which product will provide the majority of your profit?

Q How are the products produced? Do you make them to order or produce them first and then market them?

Q How unique a product/service will it be?

– To what extent will the demand for the product/service be seasonal?

– To what extent will it be a luxury or necessity item?

Q What guarantees will be associated with the product / service?

Q What is the shelf-life of your product?

Q How often do you review competitors' products or services?

Operational planning

Issues relating to operational factors might include:

Q How critical is the effective use of time to the business?

Q What technology do you use/intend to use?

– What is the condition of equipment? How does it compare with your competitors' equipment? How appropriate is the technology to your business?

Q How able are you to meet an increase or decrease in demand for your product/service?

Q How will a day's lost production due to sickness or technical failure affect output, deadlines and cashflow?

Q How have you worked out your initial capital outlay on technology?

– What is the working life of the equipment?

Q To what extent is the product/service labour intensive?

Q What emphasis are you placing on the quality of your product/service?

Hawksmere information

Hawksmere – quality programmes and practical value

Hawksmere is one of the UK s leading training organisations, providing high quality programmes allied to practical value. Every year we present around 450 public seminars as well as working with clients on a comprehensive range of in-company tailored training.

Our objective for each delegate

Our aim at every course is to provide each participant with added expertise, techniques and ideas of practical use. Our speakers are practitioners who are pre-eminent in their own field: as a result, the information and advice on offer are both expert and tried and tested.

Hawksmere offers you a broad in-depth range, from skills to strategies

Our programmes cover a wide range from management development to law, finance, insurance, government contracts and project management. They span all levels, from introductory skills to sophisticated techniques and the implications of complex legislation.

A continuing search for improvement

Our policy is to continue to re-examine and develop our successful courses, constantly updating and improving them. We offer a mixed range of one and two day public programmes, combined with some longer residential courses.

Our aim is to continue to anticipate the shifting, often complex challenges facing everyone in both the professions and industry, and to provide programmes of high quality, focused on producing practical results.

For further information on all our public seminars, call our Sales Department on 0171 824 8257.

Hawksmere In-Company

Hawksmere trainers are all professionals with sound practical experience. Our approach is participative, with extensive use of case studies and group work. The emphasis is on working with clients to define objectives, develop content and deliver in the appropriate way. This gives our client total our client involvement and support are prime contributors to the success of any programme.

As with our public seminars, participants in Hawksmere In-Company programmes will receive a customised course manual produced to our own high standard which will serve as useful reference documentation after the course.

What can we offer you?

We can provide training in all the areas covered by our public seminar programmes as well as in other topics which you may identify. In summary we can offer you:

- Tailored company programmes producing real results.

- Expert speakers matched to your company profile.

- Flexibility of time and place.

- Maximum impact on productivity through training your staff at a pace to suit you.

- Your total control over course content.

- Advice on the training needs of individuals.